The Home Book of Chinese Cookery

家常烹調

熊德達編

Thelma Lambert

THE HOME BOOK OF
Chinese Cookery

by
DEH-TA HSIUNG

with line drawings by Thelma Lambert

FABER AND FABER
London & Boston

First published in 1978
by Faber and Faber Limited
3 Queen Square, London WC1
Printed in Great Britain by
Latimer Trend & Company Ltd Plymouth
All rights reserved

© *Deh-Ta Hsiung 1978*

British Library Cataloguing in Publication Data

Hsiung, Deh-Ta
  The home book of Chinese cookery.
  1. Cookery, Chinese
  I. Title
  641.5'951   TX724.5.C5

  ISBN 0-571-11282-X
  ISBN 0-571-11283-8 Pbk.

This book is dedicated to
my Mother

ACKNOWLEDGEMENTS

I am grateful not only to my wife Thelma for all the lovely drawings in this book, but also to my father, S. I. Hsiung, for the Chinese calligraphy on the back cover and the half-title page, as well as the poem on p. 172.

D.-T. H.

Contents

Introduction

China is a vast country, about the same size as Western Europe or the United States; her climates and food products are naturally as varied as these countries. Each region has its own specialities and different methods of cooking. But there are four areas which are generally acknowledged as the principal schools of cuisine in China: Kwangtung, Huaiyang, Szechuan and Peking.

Kwangtung or Cantonese cuisine, which most overseas Chinese restaurants are supposed to serve, has the widest reputation both in China and abroad, but unfortunately most people who have ventured into one of these establishments in England or America and ordered 'chop suey' or 'sweet and sour pork' may wonder why there is any fuss at all about the art of Chinese cuisine. What they do not realise is that the dishes they have just sampled bear no relationship whatever to the kind of fare people would eat in a restaurant of similar standing in China. I shall never forget the excitement and thrill I experienced the very first time I was taken into a Kwangtung restaurant in China when I was about seven, where the speciality of the house was spare ribs in sweet and sour sauce—but what a sauce!

Huaiyang dishes from the Yangtze River Delta are of more subtle flavour, and they are also famous for their various 'pasta' dishes such as noodles and dumplings. I wonder how many Italians are aware when they eat spaghetti or ravioli that these were first brought back from China by Marco Polo in the fourteenth century?

Food from the third region, Szechuan, by contrast, is richly flavoured and piquant. The big dishes of Szechuan form an essential part of a menu at any banquet.

Finally Peking, because it has been the capital city of China for many centuries, has accumulated over the years all the best dishes from each region and thereby become the culinary centre, as well as creating a cuisine of its own.

In this book you will find dishes from all these regions, and I have selected the recipes from my own everyday meals both for the family and entertaining; but I have included nothing which is so difficult or time-consuming that only a highly skilled professional chef could be expected to produce it.

Whether you are a good or indifferent cook in the Western sense, you should acquaint yourself with some of the principles of Chinese cooking before embarking on any recipe for Chinese food. Its taste depends far more on the method of cooking, and the way it is prepared before cooking, than on the natural character of the food. The Chinese attach great importance to harmony in cooking as well as contrast in selecting the various ingredients. Another thing to remember is that cooking in China is regarded as a fine art rather than an exact science; there can never be an exact measurement of ingredients nor a precise timing for cooking a particular dish. Once you have learned the approach and a few basic techniques which are comparatively simple, the next step is experience. The details I give in the recipes are only a rough guide; after a few trials you will find a way of measuring and timing best suited to your own and your friends' tastes.

You will find that I have grouped most recipes according to ingredients and materials used rather than different methods of cooking, but I have arranged them in such a way that you can try out the simpler dishes to start off with, while the more complicated and ambitious recipes come later on in the book.

Bon appétit!

A Few Essential Points

As regards tools and materials, I have some good news for you—there are no special tools or materials required unless you want to impress your friends by producing an elaborate and complicated feast. Any ordinarily well-equipped kitchen will have all that is needed: a cutting knife and board, frying pan, oil and salt and so on. You will find that you need a very sharp knife and a rather large frying pan, and the saucepan for cooking rice should have a tight-fitting lid. The reason why you will need a sharp knife is because in Chinese cooking most ingredients are cut into small pieces beforehand, and the Chinese attach great importance to the various methods of cutting. One cookery book from China has a long chapter devoted entirely to the art of cutting and lists no less than forty-nine different ways of doing it—all using one single knife, which is a heavy cleaver. For the time being we will stick to a few basic cutting methods, using an ordinary kitchen knife. The important point to remember is that cutting before cooking introduces harmony as well as bringing out the true flavour of the ingredients. The food should be cut into units of roughly the same shape, same length and same thickness. Thinly cut food requires only a short time of cooking, and the natural flavours are thus preserved.

The basic four cutting methods are as follows:

Slicing: the ingredients are cut into very thin slices, about the size of a postage stamp, but as thin as cardboard. When slicing meat, always cut across the grain, which makes it more tender when cooked.

Shredding: the ingredients are first cut into thin slices, stacked like a pack of playing cards, and then cut into thin strips.

Dicing: the ingredients are first cut into strips as wide as they are thick, then the strips are cut at right angles in the same width so they become small cubes.

Diagonal cutting: this method is normally used for cutting vegetables such as carrots, celery or courgettes. Roll the vegetable half a turn each time you make a diagonal cut straight down.

After cutting, the next step in preparation before actual cooking is mixing—not mixing ingredients, which comes later, but what in Chinese is called 'coating': making a paste with white of egg and cornflour, then mixing in the ingredients; or mixing salt, cornflour and white of egg (in that order) with meat, chicken or fish.

The various methods of cooking can be divided into four main categories: *water-cooking*, including boiling and stewing, *oil-cooking* (frying and braising), *steam-cooking*, and *fire-cooking* (roasting and barbecuing). In China the fire-cooking method is less popular for family meals, partly because most Chinese kitchens are equipped with simple stoves but no ovens. A Chinese family expects to eat fire-cooked dishes only in restaurants.

Whichever method you choose to use, the most important thing to remember is the degree of heat. In China it is divided into 'military' (high or fierce) heat and 'civil' (low or gentle) heat. You must be able to control the heat with perfect ease, as it is vital that you should be able to turn it down or bring it up at the crucial moment; for if the heat is too high for too long, the food will be either overcooked or burnt outside and raw inside.

By far the most frequently used home-cooking method in China is quick *stir-frying*. To do this you heat up a small amount of oil in a frying-pan over a high heat, then throw in the ingredients to be constantly stirred and tossed for a short time. Timing here is of the utmost importance; overcooking will turn the food into a soggy mess. When correctly done, the food should be crispy and whole-some. Very little water or none at all is added, since the high heat will bring out the natural juices from the meat and vegetables, particularly if they are fresh. This method of cooking is very economical, since the total amount of meat and vegetables required, about ½ lb (225 g) of each, is enough for two people, or will stretch to serve four if combined with another dish. This, in days of high food prices, is a welcome economy.

The next most popular cooking method probably is *braising* or *fricassée*. You first fry the ingredients and then simmer them slowly in their own juice (braising) or in stock (fricassée).

Then comes *stewing* or what we in China call *red-cooking*; the ingredients are first fried or braised, and then stewed slowly in soya sauce, which gives colour—hence the name.

The other frequently used methods are *deep-frying* and *shallow-frying*: the first one is the same as the way chips are fried; the second is similar to that for frying eggs or sausages. As for *steaming, boiling* and *roasting*, there is very little difference from the basic methods you normally use in the West.

Your Store Cupboard

Traditionally, a Chinese housewife is supposed to check first thing each morning the following seven items in her kitchen: firewood, rice, oil, salt, soya sauce, vinegar and tea. A Western housewife is luckier in a way as she has no need to be bothered with the firewood problem, but she should add to this list sugar, pepper, cooking sherry and cornflour.

The following is a list, in alphabetical order, of the most generally used materials and ingredients. All these are obtainable from most Oriental stores (see Appendix II), or you can try your delicatessens; some of the items can even be found in a good supermarket.

Bamboo shoots: unfortunately only canned ones can be bought in the West; try to get winter bamboo shoots, which are smaller and more tender than the ordinary ones. After opening the tin, drain before use; any leftovers can be stored in fresh water in a covered jar where they will keep for weeks in the refrigerator.

Bean curd: this looks rather like white cheese, but is made from soya beans and has an unusual texture which is rather an acquired taste. Dried bean curd skin is also available in packets of sheets or sticks; this keeps for a long time, unlike fresh bean curd, which will only keep for a few days in water in the refrigerator. The dried skin is soaked overnight in cold water, or for 1 hour in warm water, before use.

Bean sauce: there are basically two kinds: yellow bean sauce and black bean sauce. They are sold in cans or jars, and are sometimes called bean paste. The yellow one is sweeter than the black one.

Bean sprouts: use fresh bean sprouts only. Canned ones should be banned by law, since they taste nothing like the real thing. Do not bother to top and tail them, as that would take you hours to do and is quite unnecessary. Just wash, rinse and discard any husks that float on the surface of the water. They will stay fresh in a refrigerator for a few days if kept in a closed plastic bag.

Chinese dried mushrooms: you only need a very small amount each time, which is just as well since they are rather expensive. Buy 2 oz (50 g) at a time: they will last you a long time and will keep indefinitely in a tightly covered jar in a cool place. Soak them in cold water overnight before use, or in warm water for about 30 minutes. Where fresh mushrooms are indicated as an alternative, the amounts suggested vary according to the nature of the recipe.

Five Spice powder: a combination of anise seed, fennel, clove, cinnamon and pepper. Use less than 1 teaspoonful at a time, as it is very strongly pungent. Sold ready mixed in plastic bags. Store in a tightly covered container.

Ginger root: sold by weight. Should be peeled and sliced or finely chopped before use. Will keep fresh for weeks in a dry, cool place.

Hoi Sin sauce: also known as barbecue sauce. Made from soya beans, flour, sugar, spices and red colouring. Sold in cans or jars. Will keep in the refrigerator for months.

Oyster sauce: a thickish, brown sauce made from oysters and soya sauce. Sold in bottles, and will keep almost indefinitely in the refrigerator.

Sesame seed oil: strongly flavoured seasoning oil sold in small bottles and will keep indefinitely.

Soya sauce: sold in bottles or cans, this sauce ranges from light to dark brown in colour, with varying strength. Will keep indefinitely.

Szechuan preserved vegetable: this pickled root vegetable is hot and salty. Sold in cans, once opened it can be stored in a tightly sealed jar in the refrigerator for months.

Tiger Lily: known as Yellow Flower or Golden Needles in China, it is a dried bud, golden yellow in colour. Has to be soaked in water before use. Will keep indefinitely.

Water chestnut: sold in cans already peeled (can be obtained fresh in the USA). Will keep for about a month in a refrigerator in fresh water in a covered jar.

Wooden Ear: also known as Cloud Ear, it is a dried tree fungus. Only a very small amount is needed for each time. Soak in warm water for 20 minutes before use.

Chopsticks and Tableware

Does Chinese food taste any better if eaten with chopsticks? This is
not purely an aesthetic question, but also a practical point too. I
think most people find it enormously satisfying to be able to use
chopsticks at a Chinese table, partly because all Chinese food is prepared in such a way that it is easily picked up by chopsticks. If you
regard eating with one's own fingers as being natural, then I always
think of chopsticks as the extension of one's fingers—only it looks
more civilised. That's why some conservative Chinese regard the
Western practice of using knives and forks as barbaric! Now you
will understand why some waiters in Chinese restaurants are so rude
to customers who use forks and spoons. Still, I myself have enjoyed
many a meal with just a fork without too much bother.

Learning to use chopsticks is quite simple and easy—use the
drawings to help you. I always maintain that using chopsticks is
like riding a bicycle: you must not concentrate too hard on what you
are doing immediately in front of you, but relax and let your mind
wander on other matters such as the beautiful person sitting next
to you, or the wonderful wine being served with the food.

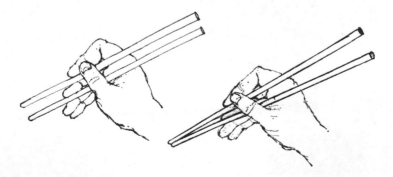

As you know, at an informal Chinese homely meal, all the dishes are brought to the table together; the host or hostess will signal the start with his or her chopsticks by waving them in the air rather like an orchestral conductor, then everybody will pick up their chopsticks and tuck in. When you think you have had enough, you simply wave your chopsticks and mutter something like 'Please don't hurry!' But in more polite society, the host and hostess will constantly serve their guests by helping them with a spoon from the centre of the table, so the guests never have to stretch out their arms to help themselves.

Anyway, one advantage of using Chinese tableware is that there is very little washing-up afterwards: all you need for each place setting is a medium-sized plate, a pair of chopsticks and a rice bowl, which doubles as a soup bowl as well when used with a porcelain spoon.

Some Useful Hints

1. Always choose the freshest vegetables you can find: do not leave them lying around too long before use. Keeping them in water may preserve the freshness of their colour, but will lose much of the vitamin content.

2. Always wash vegetables *before* cutting them up in order to avoid losing vitamins in water.

3. Cook vegetables as soon as you have cut them, so that not too much of the vitamin content is destroyed by exposure to the air.

4. Never overcook the vegetables, nor use too much water in cooking. Avoid using a lid over the pan unless specified, as it will spoil the brightness of the colour.

5. When recipes call for the use of a lid, this must be as tightly fitting as possible.

6. Do not add salt or too much soya sauce at early stages of cooking, since this will toughen the food and make it lose its natural flavour.

7. When frying fish, always start off with high heat at first, then reduce to moderate. With meat, it is the other way round: start off with moderate heat then increase it for the last stage of cooking.

8. When frying chicken or shellfish, use high heat but warm oil— too hot oil will reduce the tenderness.

9. Cornflour or any form of starch, when used discreetly, will not only preserve vitamins and protein content in meats, particularly when they are finely sliced or shredded, but also retain their tenderness and delicacy. But if they are used over-generously, the food will not only look messy, it will also taste starchy.

10. Certain kinds of vegetable oils have a strong odour: if so, heat the oil with a slice of ginger root before use.

11. It is easier to cut frozen meat into thin slices when still half-frozen; but the meat should be thoroughly thawed before cooking so as not to lose its tenderness and flavour.

12. All condiments must be used discreetly when appropriate. They should enrich the flavour of the food rather than overpower it.

I
A Very Simple Meal to Begin With

Cold sliced chicken
Red-cooked beef
Boiled rice
Stir-fried pork and green peas

Having got so far, you must be keen to make a start. Whether you are cooking for the family or close friends, you should know beforehand their likes and dislikes. One of the great advantages of Chinese cooking is that it is so flexible: even the fussiest person will normally find something to his or her liking, among a choice of three or four different dishes. Another point is the way Chinese food 'stretches', so that an extra pair of chopsticks (or a spoon and fork) is all that you need to accommodate an unexpected guest.

As a rule, allow one dish for each person if you want a biggish meal; otherwise two dishes are ample for three or even four people. Let us assume you are cooking for four people, which is a very convenient number. Here is a suggested menu:

As a starter serve cold sliced chicken, which could be prepared beforehand. This is followed by a quick stir-fried dish such as pork and green peas, which takes less than 5 minutes to cook (provided you have done the necessary preparation) and red-cooked beef together with boiled rice, both of which should have been cooked before you start the chicken dish, so there is very little last-minute panic even if you are a complete beginner.

Are you suitably tempted? Then let's get down to business.

Get a medium-sized young farm chicken (if possible fresh; frozen ones tend to be rather tasteless and tough) weighing about 2½ lb (1·1 kg). Buy ½ lb (225 g) pork fillet, which is best, or alternatively spare rib chops, which are cheaper, or any other cut of pork so long as it is not too fat; but on no account buy expensive pork chops. Then you will need 1½ lb (680 g) shin of beef; stewing beef is the next best. Next get ½ lb (225 g) fresh or frozen peas (petits pois are best if you can get them), ¼ lb (100 g) white button mushrooms, 1 lb (450 g) carrots, a bunch of spring onions (called scallions in the USA), ginger root—fresh if you live near an Oriental grocery shop, otherwise dried ginger root from delicatessens or good food shops; and soya sauce, which you can buy almost anywhere.

That will complete your shopping list, assuming your larder has cooking oil (any vegetable oil is better than fat—never use butter or dripping for Chinese cooking), salt, sherry (medium sherry is best for cooking), sugar, cornflour, eggs, and of course, rice.

Rice, as you will know, is the staple food of most Chinese. In everyday usage the Chinese words for 'rice' and 'meal' are synonymous, just as in the West the word 'bread' is used in 'give us our daily bread' or 'bread-winner'.

Cold sliced chicken

This is a famous Cantonese dish, very easy to prepare and tasty. The chicken can be cooked in the morning if it is to be served in the evening, or if you are working during the day, then do it the night before. This is the simplest dish I know and it literally requires no cooking skill whatever. What you need is a saucepan large enough to hold the whole chicken, and it must have a tightly fitting lid.

    1 farm chicken (about 2½ lb, 1·1 kg)
    2–3 spring onions
    1 tablespoon oil (sesame seed or olive)
    1 tablespoon sherry
    1 tablespoon soya sauce
    1–2 slices ginger root
    a little salt
    a little pepper

First wash the chicken thoroughly (keep the giblets for stock making), then place it in the saucepan with enough water to cover, bring it to the boil and let it simmer for 2–3 minutes only, keeping the lid very tightly shut all the time. Then remove the pan from the stove and leave it to cool; the bird will cook gently in the hot water, provided you put something heavy on top of the lid to make sure there is no escape of heat.

About 1 hour before you serve it, remove the chicken (you can either discard the water or use it as a base for making stock), cut it into small pieces and arrange them neatly on a long dish. Here a heavy cleaver is useful, or use a sharp carving-knife. Remove the bones from the chicken but try to keep the skin on.

Next mix 1 tablespoon of oil (in China one would normally use sesame seed oil, but this has a rather strong flavour which many people in the West dislike, so if you do use it, do so sparingly—just a few drops—and make up the quantity with olive oil, which can also be used by itself as a substitute), the same amount of sherry and soya sauce, a little salt and pepper, 2–3 finely chopped spring onions and a little ginger root (if you are using dried ginger root then use even less as it is sharper than fresh; but do not use powdered ginger, which has a very different flavour). Then pour this mixture all over the chicken, cover it up and refrigerate it for 30 minutes or so before serving.

Red-cooked beef

This is basically a stew, but again it can be prepared long before you serve it; in fact it always tastes better when warmed up and also gives you the chance to de-fat it when it has cooled.

$1\frac{1}{2}$ lb (680 g) shin of beef
1 lb (450 g) carrots
2 tablespoons sherry
2 tablespoons soya sauce
1 teaspoon sugar
2–3 small slices ginger root
$\frac{1}{2}$ teaspoon salt

Cut the shin of beef into $\frac{1}{2}$-in (12-mm) cubes and trim off any excess fat, but leave the sinew in the meat, as it gives the liquid extra flavour and richness. Put the meat in a saucepan with enough water to cover, add 2 tablespoons of sherry and bring it to the boil, then let it simmer for 1 hour (needless to say with the lid on), then add 2 tablespoons of soya sauce, 1 teaspoon of sugar, $\frac{1}{2}$ teaspoon of salt and 2–3 small slices of ginger root. Continue simmering for another 2 hours, but about 1 hour before serving, put in the carrots, cut into roughly the same size as the beef. They will absorb some of the fat and also give the dish a contrast in colour as well as in texture.

If you have difficulty in getting ginger root, a chopped onion or crushed clove of garlic could be used as a substitute. This method of cooking can easily be applied to cooking pork or lamb, which take slightly less cooking time.

Boiled rice

Time and again I have been asked by various people how to cook rice. The answer is very simple: you just boil it with water, there is nothing more to it than just that! Some people add salt to it, others drain it through a sieve and what have you; all this is quite unnecessary.

There are two main types of rice on sale in Britain: the long grain or Patna rice and the rounded or pudding rice. If you like your rice to be firm yet fluffy then use the long-grain type, as the rounded rice tends to be rather soft, and sticks together after cooking. Allow ¼ lb (100 g) rice per person, or ¾ lb (340 g) for four (unless you are all very hearty eaters), wash the rice in a saucepan with cold water just once, then fill the pan with more cold water so that when you put your index finger in it and let the tip of the finger just touch the top of the rice, the water level just reaches the first joint of your finger. Bring to the boil and use a spoon to give it a stir in order to prevent it sticking to the bottom of the pan when cooked. Then replace the lid tightly and turn down the heat as low as possible and let it cook for 15–20 minutes. By then it is cooked but not quite ready for serving, it is best to leave it off the heat for 10 minutes or so, as the Chinese believe that it is bad for digestion to eat rice that has only just been cooked.

Any left-over rice can be reheated by adding a little water, but a much nicer way of serving it is to fry it with a little oil and salt or soya sauce, together with an egg or two. Details will be given of this in Chapter IV.

Stir-fried pork and green peas

The very first time I visited Kew Gardens in London I was suitably impressed by the fact that many different species of trees and plants and flowers had originated in China. Imagine my amazement the other day when I discovered that the green pea, a very common vegetable in China, was actually first introduced into China from Europe during the Han dynasty (206 BC–AD 220)!

If you grow your own peas in the garden, then freshly picked, tender young peas are best, otherwise frozen petits pois are better than the discoloured, tough peas most greengrocers seem to sell. But on no account use canned peas, which have the most un-Chinese flavour for a vegetable.

½ lb (225 g) pork fillet or spare rib chops
½ lb (225 g) peas
¼ lb (100 g) button mushrooms
 1 egg white
 1 clove garlic
 4 tablespoons oil
 1 tablespoon sherry
 1 tablespoon soya sauce
 1 teaspoon sugar
 a little cornflour
 a little salt

First dice the pork into little cubes the size of large peas. If you are using spare rib chops (called shoulder slice in the USA) there may be quite a lot of fat, which you should separate and use to make lard. Mix the meat with a little salt, the white of an egg and some cornflour—not too much, just enough to cover the meat lightly. Add a little sherry and soya sauce and 1 teaspoon of sugar, then leave the meat to marinate while the button mushrooms are washed and sliced—but if the mushrooms are very small they could be left whole.

All this could be done before the guests arrive. So after you have served the cold sliced chicken as a starter, you now go into the kitchen to cook this pork dish which, as I have said, should take no more than 5 minutes in all.

Heat up the frying-pan first, then pour in about 2 tablespoons of oil. When it is hot (this will take about ¾ minute) throw in a clove of garlic, sliced into 3–4 bits—these will turn brown in about ½ minute. Discard the garlic and turn down the heat to moderate as the oil begins to smoke. Stir in the meat, using a wooden spoon or scraper to stir-fry it by constantly turning the meat until every bit is covered with the heated oil. This should take no longer than 1 minute; otherwise it will be overcooked. Put the meat back in the mixing bowl, wash and dry the pan thoroughly and heat it up over high heat again before pouring in more oil. This time heat the oil until it smokes, which will take about 1½ minutes, then empty the fresh peas or the packet of de-frosted peas into the pan, followed by the mushrooms. When the wet vegetables meet the hot oil they will make a rather loud noise, but do not be alarmed, just stir vigorously so that all the bits and pieces are covered with oil. Add some salt, continuing to stir for ½ minute or less before putting the meat back into the pan. Cook the pork and vegetables together for 1 minute longer; at this point, the ingredients should have produced enough natural juices to form a sort of gravy, but if the contents of the pan are too dry and start to burn then add a little stock or water and bring it to the boil before serving. The pork should taste crisp and tender and the appearance of the vegetables should be bright and shiny.

This is the basic method of cooking almost any food in China. Once you have mastered it, there is no end to the variations you can create by using different combinations of meats and vegetables. The two most important things to remember here are heat and timing, particularly the latter as sometimes even the fraction of a second could make all the difference. As you can see from the above instructions, the exact timing is closely related to the degree of heat, which is why it is impossible to give a precise figure; much depends on the type of stove or the thickness of the pan you use. Therefore, what I can give you can only be a rough guide. Also, as it is imperative that you should not take your eyes off the pan while cooking, let alone stare at the second hand of a clock or watch, you should really learn to time it by the appearance and sound—yes, sound; remember what I said earlier, that when you first throw the ingredients into hot oil, they will make a loud noise, but as you continue cooking, the noise will gradually become subdued; that usually is the sign that it is almost done. I suggest that just to start with you have your spouse or somebody willing to help standing by with a watch with a second hand, so that he or she could call out every 10 seconds or so.

As far as I know, no cook in China ever used a clock to time their cooking—nor any measurement for their ingredients either. What they usually do is to taste a bit from the pan while still cooking to see if it is nearly done, or if any more salt or whatever is needed. For it is comparatively simple to add more salt and continue cooking a little longer if necessary, but it would be too late if too much salt had been used or the food had been overcooked!

So now you have cooked your first Chinese meal. I am sure you have enjoyed the experience and your guests and family have probably enjoyed eating it. If they are used to the 'chop suey' type of Chinese food, they should have been pleasantly surprised to discover the home cooking of China.

A Chinese meal is served absolutely ready to eat—there is no last-minute carving on the table, nor dishing out separate items such as meat, vegetables, gravy or sauce and with all their attendant condiments; there is no long prelude when you all wait for everybody to be served before you start. At a Chinese table, when everyone is seated, the host will raise his chopsticks and say 'Chin-chin' ('Please-please')—and then you all pick up your chopsticks and enjoy yourselves.

The enjoyment of the meal would be enormously enhanced if you served wine or wines with it: as the saying goes 'Wine makes any meal into a feast'. So a few words about what to drink with Chinese food would be appropriate here.

Contrary to common belief in the West, tea is seldom served at mealtimes in China. It is true that tea is the most popular beverage of most Chinese, but it is drunk before or after a meal, or indeed during any other time of the day; at everyday lunches or suppers soup is usually served throughout the meal, and for more formal occasions or when entertaining, wines and spirits are essential parts of the fare.

To start with, a good, medium-bodied white wine such as Chablis or hock, well chilled, will serve both as an aperitif and as an accompaniment to the cold chicken. Of course if it happens to be somebody's birthday or any other celebration, champagne would be ideal, and so would a good sparkling wine—but not too sweet.

A full-bodied red wine will go best with the beef and pork dishes. Here the scope is very wide, much depends on your personal taste and of course, pocket; but as a guide, choose something which is not too heavy or sweet. I must confess that although I have a personal preference for claret over burgundy, practical experience has taught me that the latter seems to have more affiliation with Chinese food than its cousin from Bordeaux.

If there are not enough people to warrant opening two bottles, then serve a light red wine rather than white. A young, fresh Beaujolais would be most suitable, otherwise a good Côtes du Rhône or any other Provençal wine that carries a VDQS label.

Readers will notice that I have a strong preference for French wines. This is entirely personal, for wine drinking is a very personal thing. However, it does not mean that I dislike wines that are not French; far from it, for I am perfectly aware that a great many excellent wines are made all over the world, and it would be quite impossible to recommend them all here. Suffice it to say that when I mention a certain name such as Beaujolais, then Italian wines of a similar nature, such as Bardolino or Valpolicella, will do just as well, or indeed any light and refreshing wines, Californian or Australian, are equally suitable.

II
A Great Leap Forward

Lions' heads (pork meat balls)
Soya chicken
Pork and mushroom soup
Stir-fried prawns and peas
Fried beef and tomatoes
    See also:
Boiled rice (p. 28)

If I have sufficiently whetted your appetite by the previous chapter, you must be very keen to get on to the next stage and try out some slightly more complicated recipes.

This time let us take a great leap forward by cooking for six to eight people, for whom you will need at least five dishes including a soup.

As you will see from the recipes listed, this is a well-balanced menu which consists of what we in China call the three 'meats'—pork, chicken and fish. These are supplemented by other ingredients to give a contrast not only in tastes, but also in colours and textures.

Quite a few hours' preparation beforehand is required, and careful planning for the operation will avoid last-minute panic in the kitchen after the guests have arrived. But experience must have told you that no good food can come out of the kitchen without some hard work! I hope you will agree that this menu sounds very exciting, and therefore it is worth a little bit of extra trouble both to please yourself and your guests. Let's say it will be a challenge to test yourself and your skill, for if you can do these dishes well, then I assure you that nothing in this book is beyond your capability.

First, the shopping list:

½ lb (225 g) peeled prawns (or ½ lb (225 g) uncooked, unshelled
   Pacific prawns if you can get them from a good fishmonger)
1 young farm chicken (2½–3 lb, 1·1–1·4 kg)
½ lb (225 g) frying steak
1½ lb (680 g) pork (weight exclusive of bones, but it needs to be
   minced; if you have a mincer at home, then just get this amount
   of pork, either spare rib chops or any other cheaper cuts such
   as blade bone or hand (called shoulder butt or picnic shoulder
   in the USA); otherwise ask the butcher to mince most of the

pork for you, but also bring home the bones and a small un-
minced piece of lean pork about ¼ lb (100 g) in weight)

½ lb (225 g) peas (fresh or frozen, preferably petits pois)
¾ lb (340 g) hard tomatoes (under- rather than over-ripe)
¼ lb (100 g) mushrooms
1 lettuce
1 medium-sized cabbage (about 1½ lb, 680 g; ideally a Chinese
cabbage, also called Chinese leaves or celery cabbage, otherwise
a green or savoy cabbage)
1 bunch spring onions
1 ginger root

Needless to say, you will also need oil, salt, soya sauce, sugar, cornflour, sherry, eggs and rice.

Lions' heads

One of the unusual aspects of Chinese food is the fascinating names
given to most dishes. In order not to alarm any of your guests who
might be squeamish, you had better explain that the pork meat balls
are supposed to resemble the shape of a lion's head and the cabbage
is supposed to look like its mane, hence the name. When my little
daughter was offered this dish for the first time—she couldn't have
been more than four—she absolutely refused to touch it, as she had
been to the zoo earlier in the day. Later it became her favourite dish,
so much so that she doesn't allow that there could be a proper
Chinese meal without it.

1½ lb (680 g) pork
1½ lb (680 g) cabbage
1–2 spring onions
2–3 mushrooms (optional)
a few prawns (optional)
1 egg
2 tablespoons sherry
1 tablespoon soya sauce
2 teaspoons sugar
a little cornflour

a little ginger root
½ teaspoon salt
enough oil to shallow-fry in a large saucepan
enough stock or water to cover

You could start making this dish the day before if you like, but I
think it always tastes slightly better when not reheated. Allow yourself about 3 hours on the day it is to be served. First bone the pork if
it hasn't been done already, and use the bones to make a stock for
the basis of the soup. If you have brought home the pork in a whole
piece, then keep aside a small lean piece for the soup later. Now
finely mince the pork with its fat, mix it thoroughly with 1–2
chopped spring onions, a little chopped ginger root, 2–3 mushrooms,
and a few prawns all finely chopped (the mushrooms and prawns
are optional, if you are making this dish for another occasion and
you don't happen to have them in the house, then they can be
omitted), together with 2 tablespoons of sherry, 1 of soya sauce, 2
teaspoons of sugar, ½ teaspoon of salt, 1 lightly beaten egg and some
cornflour. Shape the meat into 6 round balls and put them aside.

At this stage, you should start getting other dishes ready, but
when you return to cook the lions' heads, heat some oil in a largish
saucepan, fry the cabbage, previously washed and cut in quarters
lengthwise (or in 6 or 8 bits if it is a round cabbage), stir to make
sure that all sides of the cabbage are coated with oil, then place the
meat balls on top and add stock or water to just cover the cabbage.
Bring it to the boil, then put on the lid and simmer for 30 minutes.
Alternatively, you can cook this dish in a casserole transferred to the
oven and cooked gently for 1 hour at 350° F (180° C, gas mark 4).

You can serve it from the casserole or, if using a saucepan,
arrange the cabbage in a bowl with the meat balls on top. It is
always served with rice and at the end of a meal, never as a starter.
In fact if you are cooking for two or three people only, this dish
will be ample just by itself.

Soya chicken

This dish again can be prepared the day before and eaten cold, but it
is nicer to serve it on the same day it is cooked.

1 fresh farm chicken (3–3½ lb, 1·4–1·6 kg)
1 round lettuce
5 tablespoons soya sauce
3 tablespoons sherry
1 tablespoon brown sugar
3 tablespoons oil
9 tablespoons stock or water
freshly ground pepper
finely chopped ginger root

Wash the chicken and dry it thoroughly (use the giblets to add to the pork bone soup), then rub both inside and out with freshly ground pepper and finely chopped ginger root. Marinate the bird with 5 tablespoons of soya sauce, 3 of sherry and 1 of brown sugar for at least 3 hours, turning it over now and then.

Heat 3 tablespoons of oil in a saucepan large enough to hold the whole chicken, brown it lightly all over, then add the marinade diluted with the same amount of stock or water; bring it to the boil, turn down the heat and let it simmer for 45 minutes with the lid on, turning it over several times during simmering, but being careful not to break the skin.

To serve, cut the chicken into small pieces and arrange them neatly on a bed of lettuce leaves, then pour over it a couple of tablespoons of the sauce. To add colour, you can decorate the edge of the plate with radishes or tomatoes. The remains of the sauce could be stored in the refrigerator almost indefinitely, and can be used for making a wonderful egg dish (see recipe on p. 75). If you serve this chicken dish cold, it could be a starter or as a part of the main course. It would certainly make an ideal buffet-type meal on its own.

Pork and mushroom soup

Chinese soups are mostly a clear broth to which vegetables or meats or both are added just before serving. When stock is not available, as often is the case, a Chinese housewife would simply stir-fry a small amount of greens, then add some water and soya sauce, bring it rapidly to the boil and serve it in a bowl throughout the meal.

For this dinner, we will stick to the Western convention and serve soup at the beginning. Should there be any left over, it could easily be warmed up again at the end of the meal if anybody feels like it.

> pork bones
> chicken giblets
> ¼ lb (100 g) pork
> ¼ lb (100 g) mushrooms
> 1 spring onion
> a little salt or soya sauce

Use the pork bones and chicken giblets to make a good stock, letting it simmer on a very low heat for at least 2 hours. Wash the mushrooms and cut them into thin slices lengthwise and take the small piece of lean pork kept aside from the lions' heads, also cut into thin, small slices. Now drain the stock through a strainer or sieve, bring it back to the boil and put in the mushrooms and pork. Boil rapidly for ½ minute or so. Then place a finely chopped spring onion and some seasoning (a little salt or soya sauce) in a serving-bowl, pour the boiling soup over it and stir well. Some people would add a little monosodium glutamate to give it an artificial flavour, but I do not think this is at all necessary.

Stir-fried prawns and peas

This is a very colourful dish, as well as being an excellent starter. It is very simple to make, and most of the preparations can be done long before so that it only requires a minimum cooking time.

> ½ lb (225 g) prawns
> ½ lb (225 g) peas
> 4 eggs
> 1 tablespoon sherry
> enough oil for shallow-frying
> a little cornflour
> a little salt

If you are using uncooked Pacific prawns, wash them before shelling, dry them thoroughly with kitchen paper, then use a sharp knife to make a shallow incision down the back of the prawn and pull out the black intestinal vein. Split each prawn in half lengthwise, then cut them into small pieces. Smaller, peeled prawns can be left whole.

Mix the prawns with 1 tablespoon of sherry, a little salt, 1 egg white and enough cornflour to coat them lightly. Leave them to marinate in the refrigerator for about 30 minutes.

Next beat up 3 eggs together with the yolk left over from the marinade, add a little salt and 1 finely chopped spring onion, scramble the mixture over a moderate heat in a little hot oil, then leave it to cool.

Just before serving this dish, heat some oil in a frying-pan, reduce the heat to moderate, then put in the prawns, and stir well to make sure all the pieces are separated. In less than 2 minutes, their colour should start turning pink, so quickly dish them out, for they must not be overcooked, or they will lose their tenderness. Now wash and dry the pan well before heating up some more oil, stir-fry the peas with a little salt for ½ minute, then return the scrambled egg and prawns to the pan and cook together for about 1 minute. Serve hot.

Fried beef and tomatoes

Pork is definitely the most popular meat in China, but beef is not at all widely eaten, for humanitarian reasons: for centuries oxen were traditionally the symbol of cultivation, and the Chinese people feel it would be too crude to eat the flesh of the animal which helps to feed them. My grandfather, who was a classical scholar of his time, always refused on principle to touch a beef dish. Once I watched him enjoying one at a banquet, but he insisted afterwards that he didn't know what he was eating at the time. My nanny, who was an excellent cook herself, maintained that she could tell the difference in the tastes between beef and any other meats from a mile off, and consequently she had a strong dislike for cooking beef in her kitchen, let alone eating it.

Years later, I discovered that beef was fairly commonly eaten by the Cantonese, though they tend to treat it as rather inferior to pork or chicken. This is why some Chinese restaurants in England charge less for beef dishes, even though the market prices do not reflect this trend—that's Oriental wisdom for you!

Again this is a very simple dish to make. If you have done all the preparation beforehand, then the actual cooking time should be no more than 3 minutes at the most.

½ lb (225 g) frying steak
¾ lb (340 g) tomatoes
1 spring onion
2 tablespoons sherry
1 tablespoon soya sauce
2–3 tablespoons oil
1–2 thin slices ginger root
a little cornflour
a little sugar
a little salt
a little pepper

Trim all the excess fat off the meat with a sharp knife, then cut it into as thin slices as possible across the grain. Mix it with a little salt, pepper and sugar, 1 tablespoon of soya sauce, 2 tablespoons sherry and some cornflour; leave it to marinate for at least 30 minutes.

Cut the tomatoes into ¼-in (6-mm) thick slices—do not peel off the skin, which has all the goodness in it. Finely chop the spring onion and ginger root—not too much, just 1–2 small slices. Then all is ready for the final operation.

Heat 2–3 tablespoons of oil in a frying-pan until it is bubbling, throw in the beef and stir vigorously to prevent it from sticking to the pan, and also to make sure the pieces are not stuck together. As soon as the colour of the meat changes from red to brown, scoop it out with a perforated spoon. There should still be quite a lot of oil left in the pan; if not, add a little more, wait until it smokes, then stir-fry the chopped ginger root and spring onion for a few seconds before adding the sliced tomato with a little salt. Now return the beef to the pan and cook together for about 20 seconds and serve it while it is still sizzling hot. The beef should taste so tender that it melts in the mouth, and the tomato, if you have managed to get some half-ripe hard ones, should be crisp and crunchy. Just picture the colouring on the table when you serve this dish side by side with the stir-fried prawns and peas—one brown and red, the other pink, green and yellow. You just couldn't fail to win admiration from your guests!

There are several ways of serving this meal. First, the informal, homely way in which you serve all the dishes, including soup and rice, all together, which means you make the soup first, keeping it warm while quickly stir-frying the two dishes one immediately after the other, and then serve them with the chicken and lions' heads with rice, all of which should have been ready cooked beforehand. This way the cook who these days is usually the host or hostess, can stay at the table throughout the meal, and does not have to rush out to the kitchen in between courses.

Second, the Western way in which you have the soup first, then return to the kitchen to cook the two stir-fried dishes and serve all the rest. Only after that can the cook relax and enjoy the meal with his or her guests.

Third, and this is traditionally the correct way and therefore more formal, is to serve the two stir-fried dishes first as a starter, followed by the soup, which is supposed to clear your palate for the heavier and richer food to come, which in this case are soya chicken and lions' heads with rice. Some people may find this rather strange, but I can assure you that it is very sound logic; only it is a little hard on the cook who has to jump up several times between the courses.

You will have noticed that so far I have not mentioned any sweet courses. As a rule the Chinese do not usually have any desserts to finish off a meal; they regard it as an insult to the cook if you can still eat more after a proper meal. Sweet dishes are normally eaten in between the main meals as snacks. However, for those who are used to desserts, some fresh fruit could be served as a compromise or, to be exotic, there are always such things as canned lychees, which seem to have a universal appeal.

Now about wine—see my remarks on this in the previous chapter.

This meal definitely calls for more than one bottle. In fact why not go mad and have three, since you spent such a lot of trouble over the food? I am sure you'll agree that the cook deserves it!

So, depending on which way you choose to serve the meal, I would suggest one white and two red as the safest bet. The white could be a sparkling one, which is all right for the prawn dish but not so ideal for the beef, so a better choice would be something which has not only got body but also bite, such as a Meursault or Montrachet. Both are firm, rounded wines with a fine flavour, but neither of them are cheap if you want the genuine article. For the more economically minded, why not try a white Rhône wine such as Châteauneuf-du-Pape or Hermitage? Apart from the fact that they are normally undervalued and therefore quite reasonable in price, their strength both in alcohol and flavour makes them the ideal accompaniment for a number of Chinese dishes.

Again, the scope for red wine is wide. The only thing to remember is the general rule: white before red; young before old; dry before sweet and of course, lesser wine before a greater one. '*Fay ce que vouldras*', said Rabelais more than four hundred years ago; it is still true today. The main reason why we drink wine is for sheer enjoyment; if you become too inhibited about it, then why bother? It goes without saying that your enjoyment will vary according to the occasion or setting as well as the company you are drinking with. But it is just as well to bear in mind that a claret served with seafood will taste rather metallic and thus spoil both the food and wine, while a good hock will be wasted on a richly flavoured beef dish. But pork and chicken are quite another matter: they are both so versatile that almost any wine, red or white, always tastes good with them. The only thing to remember here is that if a certain dish has a pungent seasoning such as garlic, star anise or sesame seed oil, then save your finest bottle of wine for something less spiced. Since the wine's elegance and flavour are to be overwhelmed there is hardly any point in wasting money on specially good wine.

Luckily for this particular meal, neither the soya chicken nor the lions' heads are strongly spiced, so you can literally serve any wine you like with them, provided they are good enough to do justice to your cooking. Personally, I would choose a *commune* wine from

Burgundy such as Vosne Romanée, Aloxe-Corton or Chambolle-Musigny, but claret lovers might serve a St Emilion or Pomerol. Or indeed any other wine of your personal choice, be it French, Italian, Spanish or Chinese!

III
Chicken—Variations on a Theme

Braised chicken with green peppers
Diced chicken breast with celery
Diced chicken with green peppers
Diced chicken and lychees
Chicken balls and mushrooms
Chicken slices and bamboo shoots
Diced chicken in sweet bean sauce

Hot chillis and diced chicken
Diced chicken and pork
Diced chicken with yellow sauce
Chicken wings assembly
Sliced chicken with ham and broccoli
Lotus white chicken
Long-simmered whole chicken
See also:
Cold sliced chicken (p. 26)
Soya chicken (p. 37)

III
Chicken: Variations on a Theme

Let's assume you have sailed through your big test with triumph. This must have given you a lot of self-confidence, as well as more urge to carry on with more exciting dishes. But before we go any farther, I ought to caution you not to get too over-confident about it. True enough, I did say that if you could do these dishes well, then nothing is beyond your capability. But you cannot expect to master the art of Chinese cuisine overnight, for it requires a lot of experience and practice, not just with a few dishes cooked in the simple way but literally dozens of different methods and ingredients. So before we embark on more elaborate fare, let's get down to a few more everyday homely meals.

For those who have had experience of eating Chinese food, whether in a restaurant or at a friend's home, the first thing they noticed probably was how the Chinese very seldom serve meat dishes without some kind of vegetable to accompany them. In the earlier chapters, I stressed the importance of harmony in Chinese cooking. This is achieved by a balanced selection of various ingredients in order to attain a perfect marriage between taste, colour, flavour and texture.

To start with, you first choose your main ingredient (fish, chicken or meat), then decide which type or types of vegetable will go best with it, bearing in mind the differences of colour and texture and so on. For instance, if the main ingredient is chicken, which is white in colour and tender in texture, then one would choose something soft like mushrooms or crisp like celery, or both, as the subsidiary ingredient, to give the dish a sort of harmonized texture; as an alternative, one perhaps would choose something more colourful like green pepper (crisp) and red tomato (smooth).

By combining different supplementary ingredients with the main one, you can produce almost an endless variation of dishes to astonish your family and friends; and you will find this method of cooking is very economical too, since as a rule each dish requires no more than ½ lb (225 g) each of meat and vegetables, and two such dishes should be ample for three or four people for an everyday meal. When I stayed with some friends in the South of France recently we were all appalled by the high food prices there, particularly of meat. If we had had a pork chop each—there were nine of us counting the children—it would have cost a small fortune, whereas cooking in the Chinese way we spent far less, and everybody large and small had a marvellous meal.

Braised chicken with green peppers

Another favourite practice of ours is to turn one chicken into two contrasting dishes. (This can also be done with meat: lions' heads and the soup recipe given in Chapter II are an example.)

    1 tender roasting chicken (3 lb, 1·4 kg, or more)
    ½ lb (225 g) green peppers
    2 cloves garlic
    2 tablespoons sherry
    1 tablespoon soya sauce
    water or stock to dilute these to 7 fl oz (200 ml)
    1 tablespoon sugar
    a little oil
    a few slices ginger root
    a little salt
    a little flour

Lay the chicken on its side, holding the top firmly with one hand, and use a sharp knife to cut lengthways along the curved breastbone with your other hand, slowly cutting the breast meat off the bones by following the side of the bone and the outside of the ribs. Repeat the same action on the other side and pull the meat off the bones and away from the skin, using the knife if necessary to free it. These two pieces of chicken breast you put aside for the next dish.

Now cut the rest of the chicken meat into pieces about 2 in (50 mm) square and lightly cover them with flour.

Next heat up a small amount of oil in a saucepan or a large frying-pan which has a lid, throw in 2 cloves of chopped garlic and a little ginger root, turn down the heat to moderate before putting in the chicken pieces, stir them now and again until they are brown, then add 1 tablespoon of sugar and 1 teaspoon of salt. Continue cooking while mixing 1 tablespoon of soya sauce and 2 of sherry with stock or water to make about 7 fl oz (200 ml) in all, pour this mixture over the chicken, increase the heat to bring it to the boil then reduce the heat, place on the lid and let it simmer for about 20 minutes. You have to be careful that the gravy does not run dry and allow the pieces to get stuck on the bottom of the pan— if you are using a deep saucepan, then stir the pieces of chicken once or twice to make sure they are evenly cooked. Now about 5 minutes or so before serving, stir in the green peppers, cut into pieces roughly the same size as the chicken, add a little more salt if necessary, then turn up the heat, leaving the lid off this time, and let the contents bubble a while so that there is not too much liquid left.

Diced chicken breast with celery

While the first chicken dish is being cooked, you can do this one:

    chicken breast meat (see previous recipe)
    a small head celery
    1 egg white
    1 tablespoon soya sauce
    1 tablespoon sherry
    a little cornflour
    a little salt
    enough oil for shallow-frying

Separate the meat from the white tendon and membrane of the chicken breast, dice them into little cubes, mixing them with a little salt, the egg white and a little cornflour, in that order, not all together—this is very important. Cut the celery into slices diagonally, roughly the same size as the chicken pieces. Now warm a little lard or oil and keep the heat moderate, stir-fry the chicken for a short time or until it is half-done, then scoop it out with a perforated spoon; next bring up the fire to heat the remains of lard or oil (if not enough add some more), throw in the celery, stir-fry for $\frac{1}{2}$ minute or so, pour in 1 tablespoon of soya sauce and sherry and a little corn-flour mixed to a paste with water, stir, then add the chicken and cook together for 1–$1\frac{1}{2}$ minutes, stirring all the time. Serve as soon as the gravy starts to thicken so that the meat is tender and the celery is crisp and crunchy.

With boiled rice, you should easily be able to make at least six helpings out of these two dishes; or you can make two meals out of them by serving one at a time on two separate occasions.

Naturally you don't have to buy a whole chicken in order to make these two dishes; most butchers and supermarkets will sell you chicken pieces already cut up, though their quality may not be top-grade. But if you are cooking for two or three people, you only need small quantities; otherwise it ceases to be economical.

Stir-fried diced chicken is one of the most popular dishes in China. The recipe I have just given you was passed on to me by my mother, who in turn learnt it from her mother, so you might say it is a truly traditional family recipe. Of course it goes without saying that you can easily substitute almost any kind of vegetable for the celery, all according to the season and your taste. I have come across at least half a dozen variations on this dish, all of them highly recommended. You will find them all basically very similar, and the cooking methods are the same, but it is in their varying use of supplementary ingredients and condiments that the subtle differences lie. After you have tried some or all of them, you can then decide which is your favourite. Who knows, you might even make up your own variation, by borrowing some ideas from these recipes, and that is the true spirit of Chinese cooking.

Diced chicken with green peppers

This is a Cantonese recipe. It is very colourful and delicious, but it calls for a few rather unusual ingredients which can be either omitted or substituted. If you have difficulty in finding dried mush-rooms, use fresh ones, though the flavour will be different. Canned bamboo shoots you should have no difficulty in getting from Oriental stores or even some big supermarkets, otherwise substitute with courgettes (when in season) or even young carrots.

½ lb (225 g) chicken meat
½ lb (225 g) green peppers
2 oz (50 g) bamboo shoots
½ oz (15 g) dried mushrooms (or ¼ lb, 100 g, fresh mushrooms)
1 clove garlic
1 spring onion
2 slices ginger root
1 egg white
1 tablespoon sherry
enough oil for shallow-frying
a little cornflour
a little sugar
a little salt
a little monosodium glutamate

Dice the chicken as before, mix it with the sherry and ginger root and add egg white and cornflour. Then dice the mushrooms, soaked and with the stalks removed, and also the bamboo shoots and green peppers. Chop the garlic and spring onion.

Next, warm up a little oil in a frying-pan and stir-fry the chicken for a short while. Scoop it out with a perforated spoon, then heat up the rest of the oil, throw in the garlic and spring onion, followed by the green peppers, mushrooms and bamboo shoots. Add salt, sherry, sugar and monosodium glutamate, then return the half-cooked chicken to the pan and stir-fry all together for about one minute.

You will notice that no soya sauce is used in this recipe. The question of monosodium glutamate (MSG) is a controversial one. It is a chemical sometimes known as *veh t'sin* or 'taste powder', because it is supposed to bring out the true flavour in certain foods, but it has to be used very discreetly; otherwise all dishes will have a uniform taste. A good cook in China regards it as cheating to have to resort to the use of this artificial seasoning. I remember as a child in China, I was told that because 'taste powder' was invented in Japan, it was a Japanese plot to make the entire Chinese male population sterile. So now you have been warned!

Diced chicken and lychees

Talking of sterility reminded me of another recipe which is supposed to have the opposite effect—it is traditionally given to a young person on reaching puberty as an extra boost to his or her reproductive system. It had rather a strange taste as I remember it, but then Chinese believe all good medicine should taste nasty, so you might decide to risk it. Anyway I am only including it here for your curiosity.

½ lb (225 g) chicken meat
10 oz (280 g) canned lychees
1 clove garlic
1 spring onion
a few slices ginger root
2 tablespoons sherry
1 teaspoon sugar
enough oil for shallow-frying
a little salt
a little freshly ground white pepper

Logically enough, you are only supposed to use the meat of a young cock—capon is definitely out. Dice it as for previous recipes and mix it with a little salt, sugar and cornflour, add a small piece of ginger root finely chopped, 1 tablespoon of sherry and some white pepper. While this is being marinated, cut up a few slices each of ginger root, garlic and spring onions. Now for the lychees; strictly speaking you should use fresh longans or 'dragons' eyes', a smaller variety of lychee; their flesh is firmer and therefore tastier, but unfortunately they are rather hard to come by, even canned ones, and lychees are adequate substitutes. If you can get fresh ones when they are in season so much the better. Just peel off the shells and extract the stones. Canned lychees are very easy to obtain; you should drain off the syrup and rinse in cold water. Meanwhile, mix a little water with salt, sugar, sherry and cornflour.

First stir-fry the diced chicken in a little warm oil, until done—but don't overcook. Then heat up some more oil, throw in the sliced ginger root, spring onion and garlic, stir for a few seconds, add the cooked chicken and lychees together with the prepared mixture. Mix them well and serve as soon as the liquid starts to thicken.

Well, good breeding!

Chicken balls and mushrooms

This is a more orthodox recipe—again Cantonese, and it is very simple to do.

½ lb (225 g) chicken breast meat
½ lb (225 g) button mushrooms
2–3 spring onions
1 tablespoon soya sauce
enough oil for deep-frying
a little cornflour
a little water or stock
a little salt

Use small white button mushrooms, leaving them whole. Cut the chicken into pieces roughly the same size as the mushrooms, so that when they are cooked they will look like little round balls, and mix in a little cornflour so that every single bit is covered. Heat up some oil in a frying-pan until really hot, deep-fry the chicken quickly for a very short time and scoop it out with a perforated spoon. Pour out most of the oil, heat up the remainder and then stir-fry the mushrooms and the chopped spring onion together with the chicken. Add soya sauce, a little cornflour mixed with stock or water and salt, and serve as soon as the liquid starts to thicken.

Chicken slices and bamboo shoots

This recipe originated from Shanghai, but is very popular throughout China. It is a sort of standard dish served as a starter to whet your appetite for bigger things to follow and is regarded as an ideal accompaniment to wine drinking. Also the chicken can be and often is, substituted by any other variety of meat such as pork, beef or liver, according to what is available.

½ lb (225 g) chicken meat
2 oz (50 g) bamboo shoots
¼ oz (7 g) Wooden Ears (tree fungus)
2–3 spring onions
1 egg white
1 tablespoon sherry
1 tablespoon soya sauce
1 teaspoon sugar
a little ginger root
a little cornflour
a little oil or lard
a few drops sesame seed oil

Cut the chicken meat into small slices, mix them with the white of an egg, salt and cornflour; drain and slice the bamboo shoots; soak the Wooden Ears in water (discard the hard bits at the centre) and slice them too. First stir-fry the chicken in a little warm lard or oil for about 1 minute, scoop them out with a perforated spoon; now heat up the lard or oil again, stir-fry the bamboo shoots and Wooden Ears, together with finely chopped spring onion, ginger root, sherry, soya sauce, sugar and a little stock or water. When the mixture is boiling, return the chicken to the pan, stir, add a few drops of sesame seed oil, and serve immediately.

It makes my mouth water just to think about this dish!

Diced chicken in sweet bean sauce

We are now in Szechuan, famous for its richly flavoured and piquant dishes.

½ lb (225 g) chicken meat
½ lb (225 g) bamboo shoots
2–3 spring onions
1 tablespoon sweet (yellow) bean sauce
1 egg white
1 tablespoon sherry
1 tablespoon soya sauce
1 teaspoon sugar

a little ginger root
a little oil or lard
a little cornflour
a little salt

The sweet bean sauce called for in this recipe can be substituted with plum sauce, a reddish-brown sauce with a sweet and pungent flavour, made from plums, apricots, chillis, vinegar and sugar. The chicken meat can be either breast or leg, or a mixture of both. Dice it into small cubes, mix in a little salt, egg white and cornflour.

Dice the bamboo shoots, finely chop a little ginger root and spring onion, and mix a little cornflour with soya sauce, sugar, sherry and the bean paste.

First stir-fry the chicken and bamboo shoots in warm oil, scoop them out with a perforated spoon; then heat up the oil again, stir-fry the spring onion and ginger root and add the mixed sauce together with the chicken and bamboo shoots, making sure they are well blended before serving. It should taste tender with a touch of sweetness, an ideal starter.

Hot chillis and diced chicken

This is another famous Szechuan dish that has become popular throughout China. It is reputed to have been one of Chairman Mao's favourites, because he was a native of Hunan, a neighbouring province, also known for its hot, peppery food.

½ lb (225 g) chicken meat
2 oz (50 g) fresh chillis
   (or 4 oz, (100 g) green peppers, with a little chilli sauce)
2 oz (50 g) bamboo shoots
2–3 spring onions
a little ginger root
1 tablespoon sherry
1 tablespoon soya sauce
1 teaspoon sugar
a little oil
a little cornflour
a little salt

If you cannot get fresh chillis, then use green peppers with a little chilli sauce; the general effect will be the same even though the flavour is slightly different.

After dicing the chicken into small cubes, mix them with the white of an egg, a little cornflour and salt; then stir-fry them in a little warm lard or oil for about 10 seconds and scoop them out with a perforated spoon; heat up the oil, stir-fry the finely chopped spring onion, ginger root, bamboo shoots and chillis (or green peppers and chilli sauce), then return the chicken to the pan, add sugar, sherry, soya sauce, ginger and the remaining cornflour mixture, and stir together for about 1 minute.

Diced chicken and pork

This is a Peking dish. The pork must be the tenderest fillet (called tenderloin in the USA); when cooked, its colour turns to a pale white, almost the same as chicken breast, but with a subtle difference in taste and texture.

¼ lb (100 g) chicken breast meat
¼ lb (100 g) pork fillet
2–3 spring onions
3 cloves garlic
1 egg white
1 tablespoon sherry
a little sweet (yellow) bean sauce
a little oil
a little cornflour
a little stock (or water with monosodium glutamate)
a little salt

Dice the chicken and pork into small cubes, then in separate bowls, mix them with egg white and a little cornflour. In a third bowl, mix the finely chopped spring onion (the white parts only), 3 cloves of garlic (sliced), salt, sherry, cornflour, a little sweet bean sauce and stock or water (if using water, then add a little monosodium glutamate). This is called 'yellow sauce', and should be of a rather thick consistency.

First stir-fry the diced chicken in a little warm oil or lard for a short while, and scoop it out with a perforated spoon when it is half-done. Repeat the same action with the pork; then turn up the heat and add more oil if necessary, but before the oil gets too hot, return both the chicken and pork to the pan, followed by the 'yellow sauce'; stir, and when the meats are well coated by the sauce with hardly any liquid left in the pan, the dish is ready for serving.

Diced chicken with yellow sauce

This is another Peking dish, much simpler and therefore easier to prepare.

½ lb (225 g) chicken breast meat
2 tablespoons sweet bean sauce
1 egg white
1 tablespoon sherry
1 teaspoon sugar
a little oil or lard
a few drops sesame seed oil
a little cornflour
a little monosodium glutamate
a little salt

Dice the chicken breast into small cubes, mix in the white of an egg with a little cornflour and stir-fry it in a little warm oil or lard until half-done. Scoop it out with a perforated spoon, then heat up the remains of the oil or lard, put in the yellow bean sauce first, stir, then add sugar, mixing them well; now add sherry, monosodium glutamate and a few drops of sesame seed oil. Continue stirring, and when the colour turns golden, quickly put in the half-cooked chicken; let it blend well with the sauce, and then it is ready. It should taste tender with a suggestion of sweet sauce, and the colour should be bright and glittering golden.

Chicken wings assembly

'Assembly' is a translation of the Chinese word *hui*, which refers to

food recooked in gravy thickened with cornflour. Most supermarkets sell chicken wings and legs separately. They are usually
sold 4–6 to a pack, and are very good value for money.

12 chicken wings
2–3 spring onions
1 clove garlic
2 tablespoons soya sauce
2 tablespoons sherry
1 teaspoon sugar
1 teaspoon cornflour
a little stock or water
a little oil

Trim off and discard the tip of the wings (they can be used for
making stock or soup), and cut the remains of the wings into two
pieces by breaking the joint. Mix them with 1 teaspoon each of
sugar and cornflour, 2 tablespoons each of soya sauce and sherry,
and marinate for at least 20 minutes.

Cut the spring onions into short lengths and crush the garlic.

Fry the chicken wings in a little hot oil for about 1 minute, or
until they start to turn brown, then scoop them out with a perforated
spoon. Now fry the garlic and spring onions followed by the
chicken wings, add a little stock or water, stir, then place a lid
tightly over the pan but keep the heat fairly high. Listen carefully
for the sizzling noise to make sure it is not burning. After a few
minutes add a little more stock or water and stir gently to make sure
that the chicken pieces are not stuck to the bottom of the pan, then
replace the lid and cook for a further 5–10 minutes, so that almost all
the sauce is absorbed—then it is ready to serve.

None of these chicken recipes could be called 'great' dishes, so
therefore you should not serve great wines to go with them. Since
most of them would be used as a starter—except the hot and rich
ones, which should not be served too early during the course of a
meal—a white wine would be ideal, as you can serve it as the
apéritif beforehand too. An inexpensive Loire wine, such as Muscadet, is perhaps a shade too light unless you are serving a seafood

dish as well, and the same can be said regarding German wines—they just don't seem to have enough body to sustain the rich flavour of most Chinese dishes. Leave out the great burgundies, then, and turn to the Dordogne and Alsace area for a change. You will find them dry, yet fragrant and firm. Dordogne wine is known as Bergerac, and is something between Graves and Loire; it is made from Sauvignon Blanc grapes, and represents good value compared with simply labelled 'Bordeaux Blanc' or 'Graves', which usually are rather sweet and watery. Alsace wines are named after the grape from which they are made: look out for Riesling or Traminer, both fruity and with a flowery bouquet.

Of course there is no reason why you shouldn't drink a red wine with any of these chicken dishes. Choose a light, fruity wine such as Bourgueil or Chinon, both from the Loire valley, made from the Cabernet Franc (one of the red grapes of Bordeaux). They are light-bodied, with a pronounced fruity bouquet reminiscent of summer. Naturally, a young, fresh Beaujolais would go very well too, or better still a Beaujolais with a village name such as Juliénas, Morgon or Côte de Brouilly. For claret lovers, the choice is almost limitless; I don't think you could go wrong with any of the medium-priced bottles you happen to like; if I must give an example, then any château wine not less than four or five years old from, say, Côtes de Bourg will do admirably.

The following recipes are for special occasions. They can be served on their own if there are only a small number of you, or they can form part of a feast or banquet (see Chapter IX).

Sliced chicken with ham and broccoli

This is a famous Cantonese dish which is both colourful itself, and has a rather colourful title: 'golden flower and jade tree chicken'. 'golden flower' (King-hua) is a city in South-East China which produces about the best ham in the world. (Writing in *The Compleat Imbiber* (No. 11), Henri Gault, one of the two authors of the Juillard gastronomic guides, remarked that after tasting Chinese ham, the best Parma ham seemed to taste like cardboard!) 'Jade' refers to the colour of the chicken and 'Tree', of course, to the broccoli.

1 roasting chicken (3–3½ lb, 1·4–1·6 kg)
½ lb (225 g) cooked ham (or bacon steak)
1 lb (450 g) broccoli (or asparagus or green cabbage)
2 spring onions
2 slices of ginger root
a few tablespoons chicken stock
a little oil
a little cornflour
1 teaspoon salt (and a little more)

Place the chicken in a large pan and cover it with cold water, add the spring onions and ginger root and put on the lid tightly. Bring it to the boil then reduce the heat and simmer for 3 minutes only. Turn off the heat and let the chicken cook itself in the hot water for at least 3–4 hours—you must not open the lid, which would let off the residual heat; in fact it is best to place a heavy weight on top of the pan to make sure that no heat escapes.

Meanwhile wash the broccoli in cold water and stir-fry it in a little hot oil with 1 teaspoon of salt, adding a little chicken stock if required. When it is done, arrange it around the edge of a large plate.

Now take the chicken out of the pan and carefully remove the meat from the bones but keep the skin on; then slice both the chicken meat and ham into pieces the size of a matchbox and arrange them in alternating overlapped layers on the plate that has the broccoli around it.

Just before serving, heat up a small amount of chicken stock with a little salt and thicken it with cornflour, then pour it over the chicken and ham so that it forms a thin coat of transparent jelly resembling jade.

Lotus white chicken

This is a rather complicated but not too difficult recipe. What you need here is patience; the result is most satisfying and delicious.

¼ lb (100 g) chicken breast meat
5 egg whites
3 tablespoons chicken stock (and a little more)
1 teaspoon sherry
2 teaspoons salt
1 teaspoon cornflour (and a little more)
enough oil for deep-frying
For garnish:
a few green peas
a little chopped ham

Use only the best parts of the chicken breast meat and chop it really fine until it has a creamy texture. Now mix thoroughly 3 tablespoons of stock, 1 teaspoon each of salt and sherry, 2 of cornflour and 5 egg whites with the chicken meat.

Heat a large amount of oil or lard in a frying-pan until bubbling, then gently pour a third of the chicken mixture into it. After 10 seconds or so it should start to rise to the top; gently turn it over. When its colour becomes golden, scoop it out with a perforated spoon and drain, and repeat until all the chicken mixture is cooked, then place it in a serving dish.

Heat up a little stock and thicken it with cornflour, then pour it over the chicken and sprinkle a few cooked green peas and chopped ham as garnish. Serve hot.

Long-simmered whole chicken

This is really a soup dish, but the chicken is served whole with the liquid.

Long-simmering (the Chinese term is *tun*) is a very simple method of cooking. You first plunge the main ingredient into boiling water for 2–3 minutes, then rinse it in cold water before the long-simmering starts. The purpose of this rapid boiling and rinsing process is to seal in the juice as well as to get rid of the impurities of the poultry or meat. During the long-simmering, very few supplementary ingredients—or none at all—are used, and the seasoning, which again is usually very simple, is not added until just before the completion of cooking, so that you end up with a dish of 'purity'. Because of this pure and simple method of cooking, long-simmered food is very good for invalids, or if served at a banquet ideal as a bridge-gap after several richly prepared dishes and before some more even richer food to come.

1 young chicken (about 3 lb, 1·4 kg)
1 spring onion
1 slice ginger root
1 tablespoon sherry
plenty of boiling water
a little salt

Wash and clean the chicken well before plunging it into a large pot of boiling water. Let it boil rapidly for 2–3 minutes, then take out the bird and rinse it under the cold tap thoroughly.

Now place the chicken in a saucepan or casserole that has a tightly fitting lid, add 3 pt (1·7 l) boiling water together with 1 tablespoon sherry and the spring onion and ginger root, and simmer gently over a very low heat for at least 2 hours, turning over the chicken once or twice, and at the same time removing the impurities that float to the surface.

A little salt is added just before serving. The chicken should be so tender that one can easily tear it into pieces by using one's pair of chopsticks or the soup spoon.

IV
More Vegetables than Meat

Stir-fried green cabbage
Braised Chinese cabbage
Sweet and sour cabbage
Fried spinach (also spinach with
  eggs)
Fried lettuce
Braised aubergines
Bean curd with mushrooms
Vegetarian eight precious jewels
Stir-fried four treasures
Sweet and sour cucumber
Pickled radishes
Braised eggs
Eggs with tomatoes
Fried rice

Stir-fried ten varieties
  (i)—with giblets
  (ii)—with meats
Yangchow fried rice
Fried noodles or chow mein
Noodles in soup
Vegetarian noodles in soup
Shredded pork with bean
  sprouts
Pork and french beans
Pork and cauliflower
Shredded pork with Szechuan
  preserved vegetable
Meat slices with spring onions
Shredded pork with green
  peppers
Stuffed green peppers

Stir-fried pork and mange-touts
West Lake beef soup
Pork laurel (mu-hsu pork)
Pork laurel Shantung style
Thin pancakes

See also:
Stir-fried pork and green peas
  (p. 28)
Pork and mushroom soup (p. 38)
Fried beef and tomatoes (p. 40)
Bean curd à la maison (p. 102)

True enough, I did say that no special utensils were required in order to cook Chinese food, but one implement would be very useful to have, namely the Chinese frying-pan known as the *wok*. (The correct pronunciation is *wo*; *wok* is Cantonese but is the more commonly used form in the West.)

The *wok* is cone-shaped with a rounded bottom, originally in order to fit over the round opening of a wood or charcoal stove in China. It can also be used on top of any gas or electric burners by resting it on a metal ring. The biggest advantage of the *wok* is that because of its shape, the ingredients always return to the centre however vigorously you stir them, and since the heat is evenly

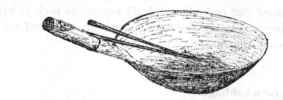

spread to all parts of the *wok*, only a short cooking time is required. The traditional *wok* is made of iron, and thus it keeps a steady and intense heat. Stainless steel and aluminium ones are less satisfactory, and also cost a great deal more. (Nowadays, you can get a *wok*, with the metal ring as optional extra, quite easily from a Chinese store.)

Don't be put off if you cannot get a *wok*; for years my mother never used one. But if you decide to get one, choose one about 14 in (350 mm) in diameter with a fitted wooden handle which is easier to manage, as you can hold it steady with one hand while you do the stirring with your other hand. A new iron *wok* should be seasoned before use. First, wash it under the hot tap, then dry it by placing it over moderate heat, and wipe the inside with a pad of kitchen paper soaked in cooking oil until clean. After each use, always wash it under the hot or cold tap; do not use any detergents, but scrape off any food that got stuck in it with a brush or nylon scourer. Dry thoroughly over a moderate heat before putting it away, otherwise the iron will rust easily.

A *wok* is very versatile; besides frying it can be used for steaming or, with a lid, for stewing and braising. For this you will find the smaller type with two metal handles is more steady when balancing on the top of your cooker. The *wok* is particularly useful when cooking fresh vegetables, like cabbage, spinach or cos lettuce, as they take such a lot of space when raw that an ordinary frying-pan, however large, will not have enough room to take a whole load without spilling them out all over the place.

There are innumerable varieties of cabbage throughout the world, the most common ones including green, white and red cabbage, brussels sprouts, cauliflower, broccoli and kale. It is interesting to note here that the Chinese word for cabbage in general, *tsai*, is the same root word that embodies all leafy vegetables such as lettuce, spinach, celery and so on. Confusingly enough, the word *tsai* also means any cooked dish.

Stir-fried green cabbage

Most people who are put off by the strong smell of boiled cabbage one often encounters in a restaurant or canteen, will be pleasantly surprised to find that if done in the Chinese way, the ordinary cabbage has a special flavour and the crunchy texture is quite different from the usual mushy bits, not to mention the fresh, natural colour that has been retained by this quick stir-frying method.

    1 small green cabbage (about 1 lb, 450 g)
    2-3 tablespoons oil
    1 spring onion
    a few peppercorns
    a little soya sauce
    a little salt

The cabbage season lasts almost all year round: from May to the end of July you have the oval-shaped spring cabbage of brilliant green; from September to February you have winter cabbage which is round with a firm heart; but in between these two seasons there are enough varieties, some early and some late, to ensure a good sequence. Choose one that is fresh, discard any outer tough leaves. Wash it under the cold tap before cutting it into thin strips like sauerkraut, and finally chop the spring onion.

Heat up a large frying-pan (or *wok*), pour in 2 or 3 tablespoons of oil, swirl it in the pan to cover most of the area, and when the oil is hot, throw in a few peppercorns; after a few seconds scoop them out before they are burnt, and discard. Now throw in the finely chopped spring onion, followed almost immediately by the cabbage, stirring constantly for about 1 minute. Add salt and soya sauce, stir a few more times, then it is done. Do not overcook, otherwise the cabbage will lose its crispness; but use as high a heat as you possibly can all the time.

Braised Chinese cabbage

Chinese cabbage is now widely available both in America and Europe, and is sometimes known as celery cabbage or Chinese leaves. It has white stalks with light green leaves, and the heart is pale yellow. One of its advantages is that it will keep fresh for a long time and its texture will retain its crunchiness however long you cook it—that's why it is so good for the lions' heads dish. However, if you cannot get a Chinese cabbage, then a hard, white Dutch cabbage can be substituted; in this case reduce the cooking time by half.

½ lb (225 g) Chinese cabbage
1 spring onion
2 tablespoons oil
a little salt

Wash the cabbage in cold water and discard any tough, tired or dry-looking outer leaves, then slice it into small pieces about the size of a matchbox.

Place a pan or *wok* over high heat, and when it is hot, pour in 2 tablespoons of oil and swirl it about in the pan; while waiting for it to smoke, finely chop the spring onion and throw it into the hot oil. Don't let it go brown, but throw in the cabbage and stir until all the pieces are covered with oil. Add salt, continue stirring; there should be enough natural juice to keep it from burning for at least 2 minutes or so. Otherwise, add a little stock or water and keep the heat high; never cover the pan with a lid while cooking.

Sweet and sour cabbage

This is originally a Szechuan dish, but has become very popular throughout China. Naturally, there are several versions as people from different regions have adapted it to their taste. This recipe is supposed to be the authentic one, as it was given to my mother by one of her friends who is a native of Szechuan.

1½ lb (680 g) white cabbage
10 peppercorns
3 small dried red chillis
3 tablespoons oil
a few drops sesame seed oil

sweet and sour sauce:
2 tablespoons soya sauce
1½ tablespoons vinegar
1½ tablespoons sugar
1½ teaspoons salt
¼ teaspoon monosodium glutamate

Choose a round, pale green cabbage with a firm heart, as fresh as possible; the white Dutch variety is a good substitute, but never use loose leafed spring greens. Wash it in cold water, and tear the leaves by hand into small pieces the size of a matchbox. Cut the red chillis into several bits, mix the sweet and sour sauce in a bowl and have it handy.

First heat the pan, then bring 3 tablespoons of oil to smoking point and throw in the peppercorns and red chillis. After a few seconds throw in the cabbage, stir until it starts to go limp—this will take about 1½ minutes—then pour in the sweet and sour sauce, continue stirring for a short while to allow the sauce to mix in well, and add a few drops of sesame seed oil just before dishing it out. It is most delicious both hot and cold.

Fried spinach

Spinach is known as Persian cabbage in China. This dark green vegetable is full of iron and therefore highly regarded for its nutritional value. The slight acid taste in your mouth when eating spinach (caused by potassium oxalate) can be somewhat reduced if you cook it in the following manner:

    1 lb (450 g) fresh spinach
    3 tablespoons cooking oil
    a little olive oil
    1 tablespoon soya sauce
    1 teaspoon sugar
    a little monosodium glutamate

If you live near an Oriental food store, you may get small fresh spinach done up in bundles (I have often come across them in Berwick Street market in London); these are much tastier than the large, pale green leaves. Wash it well and try to shake off as much excess water as possible. If using the smaller type, keep the red root, as it adds colour as well as flavour.

Heat up the *wok* or a large saucepan (no ordinary frying-pan is big enough to hold all the raw spinach leaves), pour in at least 3 tablespoons of oil, swirl it around until it covers almost the entire pan, and heat it until it smokes. Stir-fry the spinach for about 1 minute, add 1 tablespoon of soya sauce and 1 teaspoon of sugar, mixing well, followed by monosodium glutamate and a little olive oil; stir a few times more, then it is ready to serve.

This is really the basic method of cooking all types of fresh vegetables in China; of course the soya sauce can be substituted by salt, or the adding of monosodium glutamate and olive oil can be omitted.

Another popular way of serving spinach is to combine it with 2–3 scrambled eggs: cook the eggs first, then add them to the spinach at the last stage. If you garnish this dish with a few slices of cooked ham, then it becomes really colourful as well as having an even better flavour.

Now if you serve this dish with some boiling water, then it becomes an instant soup. In fact, you can apply this simple method of soup making to many Chinese recipes—see my remarks under 'pork and mushroom soup' (p. 38).

Lettuce was first introduced into China from Europe in the sixth or seventh century, and was regarded as a luxury item at first. Nowadays it is widely grown and has since become an everyday vegetable throughout the country.

There are two main varieties of lettuce: the round cabbage and the long cos—I have never come across Webb's lettuce in China. While lettuce is almost always used as a salad vegetable in the West it is seldom eaten raw in China; perhaps you would like to try the following recipe for a change:

Fried lettuce

The upright cos lettuce with crisp leaves is best for this method of cooking—if you use cabbage lettuce, then you will need more than one.

    1 large cos lettuce
    2–3 tablespoons oil
    a little salt

Wash the lettuce in cold water and discard the tough outer leaves; tear the larger leaves into halves—never use a knife to cut them—and lightly shake off the excess water as you would when making salad.

Heat up a large frying-pan or *wok*, pour in 2–3 tablespoons of vegetable oil, and let it smoke before throwing in the wet lettuce. This will make a loud noise; do not be alarmed, but stir vigorously until all the leaves are coated with oil, just as you would when mixing salad dressing. Then add a little salt and stir a few times more; by then the noise will be subdued and the lettuce leaves become slightly limp. Quickly dish it out and serve.

Make sure you do not overcook, otherwise the lettuce will lose its crispness and bright green colour.

Braised aubergines

Although the aubergine (eggplant) originated in India, it is very common and popular in China. It is one of the very few vegetables that require a longer cooking time than usual.

½ lb (225 g) aubergines
1–2 spring onions
2 slices ginger root
1 pt (570 ml) oil
¼ pt (140 ml) stock
1 tablespoon sherry
1 tablespoon soya sauce
a little sugar
a little monosodium glutamate

Choose the long, purple variety of aubergine rather than the large, round kind if possible. Wash in cold water and discard the stalks. Cut the aubergines into diamond-shaped chunks (always cut aubergines just before cooking, otherwise the white flesh will darken in colour). Heat up a lot of vegetable oil (at least 1 pt (570 ml)) in a pan, and before it gets too hot, deep-fry the aubergine pieces for about 1½ minutes, that is, until the oil starts to bubble and the aubergine starts to change its colour and texture; then scoop it out with a perforated spoon and drain.

Leave about 1 tablespoon of hot oil in the pan, throw in the finely chopped spring onions and ginger root with ¼ pt (140 ml) stock, add the aubergines, sherry, soya sauce, and a little sugar, stir and bring it to the boil, then put the lid on and reduce the heat. Simmer for a further 1½ minutes, open the lid and increase the heat again, stir for a few seconds, and now add a dash of monosodium glutamate and a little more of the oil if necessary. Shake the pan a few more times—by then the juice should be reduced to almost nothing —and serve.

Bean curd with mushrooms

This is a purely vegetarian dish. It is very refreshing and therefore most welcome when served as the last course after a big and rich feast.

> 4 cakes bean curd (see notes on bean curd, pp. 16 and 102)
> 3–4 medium-sized Chinese dried mushrooms (or 2 oz, 50 g, fresh mushrooms)
> 1 tablespoon sherry
> 1 tablespoon soya sauce
> enough oil for shallow-frying
> 1 teaspoon cornflour
> ½ teaspoon salt
> ½ teaspoon sugar
> a little monosodium glutamate
> a little sesame seed oil

Soak the dried mushrooms in warm water for about 30 minutes, squeeze them dry and discard the stalks—but keep the water for use as stock. Slice each square of bean curd into ¼ in (6 mm) thick slices, then cut each slice into 6 or 8 pieces.

First stir-fry the mushrooms in very hot oil for a short while, then add about ¼ pt (140 ml) of the water in which the mushrooms have been soaking. Bring to the boil and add the bean curd with ½ teaspoon each of salt and sugar; let it bubble for a while, then add a dash of monosodium glutamate, 1 tablespoon of sherry and a few drops of sesame seed oil. Finally, mix 1 teaspoon of cornflour with 1 tablespoon of soya sauce and a little water, pour it all over the bean curd, so that it forms a clear, light glaze, and serve immediately.

Vegetarian eight precious jewels

Unlike most of his counterparts in the Western world, the Chinese vegetarian is strictly not supposed to touch anything remotely connected with animals, not even eggs or milk; he can only eat purely vegetable matter. In order to make their diet a little more exciting, the monks and nuns and other Buddhist vegetarians invented a special cuisine in China, including vegetarian dishes that simulate meat not only in texture and appearance, but in flavour as well.

Naturally, these vegetarian foods require special skill and ingredients which are beyond the scope either of this book or of its author. However, one of their best-known dishes is known as eight precious jewels. I have adapted it for Western kitchens, since some of the original ingredients are rather hard to come by.

4–5 dried mushrooms (or 2 oz, 50 g, fresh mushrooms)
½ oz (15 g) dried bean curd skin
½ oz (15 g) dried Tiger Lily
½ oz (15 g) Wooden Ears
2 oz (50 g) bamboo shoots
2 oz (50 g) carrots
2 oz (50 g) Chinese cabbage (or celery)
2 oz (50 g) broccoli (or any green vegetable such as french beans
4 tablespoons oil
a little soya sauce
a little monosodium glutamate
a little salt
a few drops sesame seed oil

Soak all the dried vegetables separately in cold water overnight or in warm water for about 1 hour, and slice them into thin strips, except the Tiger Lily which is in small strips already. Slice the bamboo shoots, cabbage, carrots and broccoli. Heat a large pan; when it is hot put in about 2 tablespoons of oil and wait till it smokes. Stir-fry all the dried vegetables together with the bamboo shoots, add a little salt and the water from the dried mushrooms, bring it to the boil for a few seconds then dish it out. Now wash the pan and heat up some more oil, stir-fry the carrots, cabbage (or celery) and broccoli (or greens) with a little salt for about 1 minute, then add the partly cooked dried vegetables with a dash of monosodium glutamate and a little soya sauce. Continue stirring for another minute; if the contents start to go dry, add a little more water to keep them from getting burnt. Add a few drops of sesame seed oil before serving. If you like, this dish can be served cold.

Stir-fried four treasures

This is a simplified variation of the eight precious jewels dish, rather like the mixed vegetables you get in a frozen packet, but with a difference.

- ¼ lb (100 g) sweet corn
- ¼ lb (100 g) peas
- ¼ lb (100 g) carrots
- ¼ oz (7 g) Chinese dried mushrooms (or 2 oz, 50 g, fresh mushrooms)
- 3 tablespoons oil
- 1 tablespoon sherry
- a little soya sauce
- a little monosodium glutamate
- a little salt

Soak the mushrooms in warm water for 30 minutes and dice them into small cubes the size of peas. If using fresh mushrooms, try to get the smallest white button mushrooms and leave them whole; otherwise cut them into small pieces. Also cut up the carrots.

Heat up 3 tablespoons of oil in a frying-pan. Stir-fry the mushrooms first, followed by the sweet corn and carrots. Add a little salt, sherry and the water from the mushrooms, and when the liquid is almost absorbed, put in the green peas with a little soya sauce and monosodium glutamate. Stir all together for about 1 minute, then it is ready to serve.

Sweet and sour cucumber

Cucumbers have been widely cultivated in China for more than two thousand years, since their introduction from India where they originated. There are a number of species on the market, but the most common one is dark green with a smooth skin and about 1 ft (300 mm) in length. This vegetable, although very watery, is eaten cooked as well as raw.

1 medium-sized cucumber
3 tablespoons sugar
2 tablespoons vinegar
a little salt

Split the cucumber in half lengthways then cut it across into thin slices. Extract its bitter juice by marinating it with a little salt for 10 minutes or so, then pour the juice away. After that mix it thoroughly with 2 tablespoons of vinegar and 3 tablespoons of sugar, and then it is ready to serve.

Pickled radishes

2 bunches radishes
2–3 teaspoons sugar
1 small teaspoon salt

Choose radishes that are roughly equal in size if you possibly can, and discard the stalks and tails. Wash them in cold water and dry them well. Now use a sharp knife to make several cuts on each of the radishes about two-thirds of the way down but not all the way through.

Put the radishes in a large jar. Add 1 small teaspoon of salt and 2–3 teaspoons of sugar, shake the jar well so that each radish is coated with the mixture. Leave them to marinate for several hours or overnight. Just before serving pour off the liquid and spread out each radish like a fan, either on a plate or on a garnish with other cold dishes, such as braised eggs.

Braised eggs

6 eggs
sauce to cover (see below)

If you have tried out the recipes for soya chicken (p. 37) or fragrant pork (p. 104), then you should have some sauce left stored in the refrigerator. The best result for this egg dish would be to use a mixture of both sauces; otherwise either one will do.

The method is very simple; all you have to do is to hard-boil 6 eggs in water for 5 minutes or so, then carefully remove the shells and simmer them in the sauce over a gentle heat for 20 minutes or so, turning the eggs over now and again if there is not enough sauce to cover them all.

Leave the eggs to cool in the liquid, and just before serving take them out and cut them into halves or quarters. Arrange them on a plate either on their own or decorated with pickled radishes.

Eggs with tomatoes

The tomato is a native of South America and was not introduced into China until the end of the last century. Ideally you should use green, hard tomatoes for this recipe, but if you do not grow your own or are unable to find them on the market, then choose the most under-ripe and hard ones possible.

½ lb (225 g) tomatoes
4 eggs
1 spring onion
enough oil for shallow-frying
a little salt

Cut the tomatoes into slices. Finely chop the spring onion and add it to the eggs with a little salt, then beat the mixture till frothy.

Heat the oil until it smokes and throw in the tomatoes, then almost immediately pour the eggs over the tomatoes. Remove from the fire as soon as the eggs begin to harden. Serve hot.

Fried rice

4 teacups cooked rice (for 4 people)
2 eggs
1 spring onion
some left-over cooked meat or vegetables (optional)
a little soya sauce
a little oil

To use up any left-over cooked rice (allow 1 teacup at least for each person) the best way is to stir-fry it in a little hot oil over a moderate heat. When all the grains are separated, add the two beaten eggs, continue stirring, then add a little soya sauce and finely chopped spring onion. If you happen to have any left-over cooked meat such as chicken, pork, or ham, or vegetables such as peas, carrots, or green pepper, this will not only improve its texture but its appearance as well.

As I said earlier, stir-frying is by far the most frequently used cooking method in a Chinese home; practically all fresh vegetables are cooked in this way. After you have perfected your skill at this comparatively simple technique (heat and timing are the essentials), aided by a little experimental spirit and imagination, you should be able to turn almost any ingredient into a successful dish without sticking strictly to the recipes, and thus you can produce 'more than 57 varieties' with ease.

For the time being we will stick to a few more homely dishes, mostly done in the quick stir-frying manner and using ingredients easily obtainable such as pork, beef, chicken, fish, eggs and any fresh vegetable that happens to be in season, as well as a selection from your store cupboard.

Any of these dishes should serve at least two people on its own, or it will stretch to four or five helpings if combined with another dish. Suppose you have prepared three different dishes for five people, and at the end you find that there was a small portion left in each of the dishes. Don't think they will be wasted; if you warm them up the next day by mixing them all together, you will have created your own 'chop suey', for that is precisely what a genuine chop suey should be—a hotch-potch of left-overs.

I wonder how many readers realize that the type of chop suey dishes one gets in a Chinese restaurant in Europe or America is quite alien to the Chinese? There are several accounts of the origin of this most popular 'Chinese' dish outside China. According to my father, how it happened was like this: when the first-ever Chinese restaurant was opened in San Francisco over a hundred years or so ago, not a single person would dare to go in to try out this exotic eating place, and consequently there was quite a lot of ready-prepared food left over day after day. Finally, one courageous American, a drunken sailor, my father thought—staggered in and demanded the specialities of the house. The astonished cook, who was most probably asleep, quickly produced a mixture of whatever was at hand. Obviously the customer had never tasted anything like it in all his life, and wanted to know what he was eating. The equally surprised proprietor, who was a seaman himself, racked his brains and came out with the truth, and called the dish *tsa-sui*, which literally means 'miscellaneous fragments', or to put it in simpler terms 'mixed bits'. Thus the world-famous chop suey was born.

If this story were true, that cook did not so much create an original dish as merely use his wits and do what any Chinese housewife would have done in the same situation when an unexpected guest called; but to actually serve a dish of left-overs in a restaurant was unheard of. In a sense, that cook unwittingly invented a new dish that was to become the symbol of Chinese restaurants abroad.

Stir-fried ten varieties (i)—with giblets

In China, the Chinese have their own mixed dish, which is known as *shih-chin*: this means 'ten varieties', though it may not always consist of ten different ingredients, nor should they all be left-overs. Indeed, all the ingredients are specially selected in order to achieve a perfect balance of texture, colour and flavour. The dish should have a distinct taste and never be a jumbled mess like the type of chop suey one gets from most takeaway places.

Giblets from one or two chickens (or ducks)
3 or 4 Chinese dried mushrooms
1 small can bamboo shoots
6 oz (170 g) green peas
2–3 spring onions
2 tablespoons soya sauce
1 tablespoon sherry
2 tablespoons oil
a little stock or water
a little cornflour
a little salt

In cooking terms, giblets means the head, neck, heart, pinions, feet, gizzard, kidneys and liver of poultry. These are normally used for making stock or, more often than not, discarded by people who do not know what to do with them. This is a pity because they not only have a high nutritive value, but can be made into excellent dishes; in China giblets are regarded as a delicacy.

For our dish, we only need to use the gizzard and liver. The gizzard requires thorough cleaning and trimming. Make sure the gall bladder is not broken when removing it from the liver; otherwise it will leave a sharp bitter taste. Now cut them into small pieces, and mix them with a little soya sauce, sherry and cornflour. Soak the mushrooms in warm water for about 30 minutes, squeeze them dry and cut them into small pieces, and also cut up the bamboo shoots and spring onion. Mix in a separate bowl a little stock (or water) with 1 tablespoon of soya sauce and cornflour.

To cook, first heat a large frying-pan, pour in about 2 tablespoons of oil, swirl it about in the pan until it smokes, and stir-fry the mushrooms, bamboo shoots, green peas and spring onion with a little salt for about 1½ minutes. Keep them on a warm plate while washing the pan, then heat up some more oil and stir-fry the giblets for about 1 minute before returning the cooked vegetables to the pan; continue stirring, then add the stock mixture and stir for a few seconds until all the ingredients are coated with a light, clear glaze. Serve it immediately. Besides all the different flavours and textures, you should get a very colourful dish, combining green, white, black, brown and purple.

Stir-fried ten varieties (ii)—with meats

¼ lb (100 g) cooked chicken meat
¼ lb (100 g) cooked ham
2 oz (50 g) prawns (peeled and cooked)
3 Chinese dried mushrooms
1–2 bamboo shoots
¼ lb (100 g) green peas
3 eggs
1 tablespoon sherry

a little soya sauce (optional)
enough oil for shallow-frying
a little salt
a little chopped spring onion for garnish (optional)

This is an ideal way of using up left-overs from roast chicken and ham joints. Otherwise get a quarter-portion of ready-cooked chicken and dice it into small cubes. Do the same with the ham, mushrooms and bamboo shoots. Stir-fry all these together with the prawns and the green peas for about 1 minute, add a little salt and sherry, then keep it aside while you heat some oil, beat up the eggs with a little salt and make an omelette, but break it into small pieces before it is set hard. Now return all the other ingredients to the pan and cook them all together for a few more seconds before serving. This dish is even more colourful than the previous one, as it has the additional colours of yellow (egg) and red (ham).

This is a very good starter or an excellent accompaniment to wine (both red and white). But if you happen to have some ready-cooked rice handy, then you can turn it into a meal on its own, or as a part of a buffet-type meal.

In this case proceed as before, but when you have cooked the beaten eggs, keep them aside with the rest of the ingredients. Now heat up some more oil and reduce the heat when it starts to smoke, stir-fry the cooked rice until all the grains are separate, add a little soya sauce, stir, then return all other ingredients and cook all together until they are well mixed. If you like, garnish it with a little finely chopped spring onion when serving.

This is a superior variation of fried rice you can get from most Chinese restaurants, known as Yangchow fried rice, and is very popular, particularly among young people. Of course you can omit the mushrooms or bamboo shoots, or indeed substitute them with any left-overs you happen to have in your kitchen. Just use your ingenuity and make your own blend of ten varieties.

Yangchow fried rice

This is a Cantonese dish, but it must have originated from Yangchow, which is almost a thousand miles away in the Yangtze River delta.

As you can well imagine, there are several variations of this recipe. The one given below is only a basic one from which you should be able to substitute or vary the ingredients as you wish.

¼ lb (100g) prawns
2 oz (50 g) ham
¼ lb (100 g) green peas
3 eggs
2 spring onions
1 cucumber
4 teacups cooked rice
3 tablespoons oil
a little cornflour
a little salt

Use peeled and cooked prawns; mix in a little salt, 1 egg white and cornflour. Next dice the ham into small cubes the size of peas, finely chop the spring onions and cut the cucumber into thin slices.

First heat 1 tablespoon of oil in a large frying-pan, and while waiting for it to smoke, beat up 2 eggs with the yolk left from the first egg together with a pinch of salt and spring onion. Make an omelette and put it on a plate to cool while you heat up some more oil in the pan over a moderate fire. Quickly slice the omelette into thin strips. Now stir-fry the prawns in warm oil for about ½ minute, bring up the heat, add green peas and ham and cook together for 1–2 minutes more, then dish it out on to a warmed plate. Next wash the pan and heat up more oil; when it smokes reduce the heat and stir-fry the rice until each grain is separate, then return the prawns, peas, ham, and omelette to the pan and mix them well. Garnish with a little spring onion, and decorate the edge of the plate with cucumber slices.

Fried noodles or chow mein

After chop suey, chow mein (which means 'fried noodles') must be the next most popular 'Chinese' dish to a Westerner—apart, perhaps, from sweet and sour pork. Curiously enough, although noodle dishes are widely eaten in China, the famous 'crispy' noodles served in most Chinese restaurants abroad are just as alien to the Chinese as chop suey. How this came about is a complete mystery to me.

However, fried noodles can be very good when properly done. It is very quick and simple to cook, also it calls for no special supplementary ingredients once you have got the basic material. As with the ten varieties dishes, you could use almost any left-overs to improve its flavour and texture.

½ lb (225 g) egg noodles or spaghetti
¼ lb (100 g) meat (pork, beef or chicken)
1 bamboo shoot
¼ lb (100 g) leaf spinach
1 tablespoon soya sauce
1 tablespoon sherry
enough oil for shallow-frying
a little stock or water
a little sugar
a little cornflour
a little salt

If you cannot get Chinese noodles, then use spaghetti (or the finer spaghettini) or flat noodles. Allow at least 2 oz (50 g) per person. But if you are lucky enough to live near an Oriental store or Italian delicatessen, you may be able to get freshly made noodles, which would taste even better.

First shred the meat into small, thin strips, and mix in a little soya sauce, sherry, a dash of sugar, and cornflour. Then shred the bamboo shoot into thin strips, and wash the spinach leaves if fresh ones are used. Now cook the noodles in boiling water according to the instructions on the packet; normally this would take about 5 minutes, but freshly made noodles will only take about 2 minutes or less—be careful not to overcook them, or they will become soggy. Meanwhile, heat a little oil in a frying-pan, stir-fry the meat and vegetables together with a little salt for about 1½ minutes, and add a little stock or water mixed with cornflour to make a thickish sauce. Reduce the heat, quickly drain the noodles in a sieve and add them to the frying-pan, mix them well with the sauce and serve hot.

This is a basic recipe for chow mein, and it never fails to please

eager eaters, big and small—it is a firm favourite with both my
daughters and their friends. Of course you can substitute any of the
ingredients as you like: for instance, the meat could be beef, ham,
chicken or prawns, the vegetables could be cabbage, lettuce or
cucumber, cauliflower, green peas, broccoli or asparagus. The thing
to remember here is the contrast of texture and colour.

Noodles in soup

In China, noodles are served in soup (the name for this is *tang mein*)
far more commonly than fried. Why this should be so is hard to explain. On the surface, there is little difference in ingredients used in
both dishes, and the methods of preparation are practically identical
until the last stage. The recipe given below again is a basic one, you
can alter it to suit your preference or according to what is available.

½ lb (225 g) egg noodles or spaghettini
¼ lb (100 g) meat (chicken, pork, ham or prawns)
1 bamboo shoot
3 Chinese dried mushrooms (or 2 oz, 100 g, fresh mushrooms)
¼ lb (100 g) leaf spinach (or 1 lettuce heart)
1 spring onion
¾ pt (425 ml) chicken broth or stock
1 tablespoon soya sauce
1 tablespoon sherry
enough oil for shallow-frying
a little sugar
a little cornflour
a little salt

Cut the meat into thin shreds and marinate in a little soya sauce,
sherry, sugar and cornflour as for the previous recipe. Soak the
dried mushrooms in warm water for about 30 minutes (or substitute
fresh mushrooms), shred them and the bamboo shoots, wash the
spinach leaves, and finely chop the spring onion.

Cook the noodles or spaghettini as directed, and at the same time
warm up some chicken broth or make a stock by using a chicken
cube. Next stir-fry the meat and vegetables (minus the spring onion)

as for chow mein, only this time instead of mixing everything together in the frying-pan, just drain the noodles and place them in a
large serving-bowl, then pour the boiling stock or broth over the
noodles until they are almost covered. Finally, pour the meat and
vegetable mixture on top, garnish with finely chopped spring onion
and serve immediately.

Strictly speaking, you are not supposed to serve either of the noodle
dishes at a main meal, and definitely not at the same time as rice—
just as you would not serve chips and spaghetti together. Noodle
dishes in China are normally served in between meals as a snack.
Traditionally though, they are always served at birthday celebrations, partly because the length of noodles represents long life to a
Chinese mind.

Noodles in soup are sometimes used for medicinal purposes: I
remember on many an occasion, as a child in China, when I had a
cold my nanny would cook me a large bowl of vermicelli—fine
noodles—in steaming hot vegetable soup with masses of ground
pepper. It had a sharp taste and my eyes would be streaming with
tears. But I would always feel much better afterwards. I suppose it
had the same effect as an old-fashioned mustard bath!

Vegetarian noodles in soup

My earliest recollection of the Chinese countryside is of a trip to a
Buddhist temple high up in the wooded hills a few miles from
Nanchang, my grandparents' home town south of Yangtze River. I
was about four or five at the time, and my parents had just returned
from Europe after an absence of two years or more. There was an
atmosphere of joyousness and festivity—it might well have been at
the time of Chinese New Year. It was customary to pay a visit to a
temple both before and after a long journey, as well as during the
New Year celebrations, not so much for religious worship but rather
out of a sense of duty, and to carry on the tradition.

What I remember most vividly to this day is not so much the
beautiful scenery which was to become very familiar later on in my
life, but the delicious vegetarian noodles in soup the monks offered

to their guests on that occasion. It tasted quite unlike anything I ever had before, and totally different from what my nanny used to give me for my colds. Imagine my amusement when thirty years later, and more than ten thousand miles away in London, I was looking through an old manuscript in the British Museum Library, and I came across this recipe.

½ lb (225 g) fine noodles, preferably vermicelli
½ oz (15 g) dried bean curd skin
3 or 4 Chinese dried mushrooms
½ oz (15 g) dried Tiger Lily
2–3 tablespoons oil
1 tablespoon soya sauce
a little cornflour
a little sugar
a little salt
a little monosodium glutamate
a few drops sesame seed oil

Soak the dried bean curd skin in cold water overnight or in warm water for about 1 hour and slice into thin strips; do the same with the dried mushrooms; but Tiger Lily needs no slicing as it is in thin strips already. Keep the water in which all these have been soaked for use as stock.

Place a frying-pan over a high heat; when it is hot, put in 2–3 tablespoons of oil and wait for it to smoke before stir-frying the bean curd skin, mushrooms, and Tiger Lily for a few seconds. Add salt, sugar and a dash of monosodium glutamate; continue stirring for a few more seconds, add the stock mixed with a little cornflour and soya sauce, bring it to the boil, turn down the heat and let it simmer gently while you cook the noodles in boiling water for about 2 minutes. Drain the noodles and place them in a large serving-bowl, quickly pour the entire contents of the frying-pan over the top. There should not be too much soup—only just enough to half-cover the noodles. Add a few drops of sesame seed oil before serving.

According to my source, this dish was offered to the Emperor of China on each New Year's Day—traditionally a fasting day. I daresay after the rich feasts he had had all the year round, this simple dish must have been a welcome change for his digestive system!

Those who have been to a 'chop suey' type of Chinese restaurant will have found that almost every single dish served there contains the ubiquitous bean sprouts. It is true that bean sprouts are one of the most common ingredients in China since they are not seasonal, but they are normally regarded as an everyday, homely type of food, which one would not expect to find on the menu of a restaurant, however humble, except as an ingredient in a few particular dishes. The only explanation I can offer for their popularity abroad is that perhaps in earlier days, when authentic Chinese food was rather hard to come by, bean sprouts were so easy to grow that the restaurant cooks, who were no skilled professional chefs in the strict sense, had to rely heavily on bean sprouts to give their dishes the exotic touch that most customers expected. Thus it became a kind of vicious circle, which continues to this day.

What amazes me is that even though fresh bean sprouts are readily available almost everywhere nowadays—thanks to the flourishing of 'chop suey' Chinese restaurants—most cookery writers still advise their readers to use canned bean sprouts in their recipes. This is unforgivable, as it is easy to grow your own if you cannot get them fresh from your local supermarket.

Although I must confess that I have never attempted growing them myself (the need never arose), I have often sampled excellent bean sprouts grown by my mother and her friends. You can obtain packets of mung beans from many shops and health food stores, with detailed instructions.

Shredded pork with bean sprouts

I must emphasise again that on no account should you use canned sprouts, which do not have the crispness of texture which, apart from their high content of vitamin C, is the main characteristic of fresh sprouts.

½ lb (225 g) fresh bean sprouts
¼ lb (100 g) pork

1 tablespoon sherry
1 tablespoon soya sauce
1 teaspoon sugar
enough oil for shallow-frying
a little salt

Wash and rinse the bean sprouts in cold water and discard any husks that float to the surface. Shred the pork into thin strips and stir-fry it in a little heated oil; when the colour of the meat changes, add soya sauce, sherry and sugar, mixing well, and when the juice starts to bubble, dish it out and put it aside.

Next wash the pan and heat up some more oil; this time wait for it to smoke, then put in a little salt, followed by the bean sprouts. Stir vigorously so that every bit of sprout is coated with oil. Now return the pork to the pan and cook all together for about 1 minute, stirring constantly. When the bean sprouts start to appear transparent, and the juice starts to bubble, then it is done, for even slight overcooking will make the sprouts lose their crispness.

Pork and french beans

French beans (*haricots verts*), also known as string beans, were introduced into China many centuries ago. They have a most delicate flavour; try to get them as fresh as you possibly can—if you grow your own, then pick them at the last moment. Of course, runner beans can be substituted.

½ lb (225 g) pork
½ lb (225 g) french beans (or runner beans)
1 tablespoon soya sauce
1 tablespoon sherry
1 teaspoon sugar
enough oil for shallow-frying
a little cornflour
a little salt
a little water or stock

Wash the beans first; provided they are fresh and young they will not be stringy, and therefore need only be topped and tailed. If using dwarf beans, leave them whole; larger ones should be snapped in half; if using runner beans, they should be sliced. Cut the pork into small slices too, and mix them with a little soya sauce, sherry, sugar and cornflour.

Heat up some oil in a pan, and before it gets too hot, stir-fry the pork for about 1 minute or until the colour of the meat changes, then dish it out and keep it aside.

Now wash and dry the pan, heat up some more oil, but this time wait until it smokes before frying the beans with a little salt; stir constantly for about ½ minute, then return the pork to the pan and blend it well with the beans. Add a little stock or water if necessary, but do not overcook or the beans will lose their crispness and the pork its tenderness.

Pork and cauliflower

According to *Larousse Gastronomique*, the cauliflower is Oriental in origin and has been known in Italy since the sixteenth century. But the interesting thing about this is that I was positively told in China that cauliflower was European in origin and was only introduced into China in the seventeenth century. So who is right? Maybe Marco Polo had something to do with this confusion. Anyway, cauliflower as a vegetable is highly regarded in China and is widely cultivated. Oddly enough, the purple variety, broccoli, which personally I much prefer, is less popular in China.

¼ lb (100 g) lean pork
1 medium-sized cauliflower
1 tablespoon soya sauce
1 teaspoon sugar
enough oil for shallow-frying
a little cornflour
a little monosodium glutamate
a little salt

When choosing cauliflower, make sure the leaves that curl round the flower are bright green and not withered—in this way you can tell that it is fresh. Keep a few leaves on when cooking, as they add to the colour and flavour. First wash the cauliflower under cold water, and cut the flower into sprigs with part of the stalk still attached. Slice the pork and mix it with the soya sauce, sugar and a little cornflour.

Heat up some oil and stir-fry the cauliflower sprigs with a little salt and monosodium glutamate for about 1½ minutes, adding a little stock or water; let it bubble for a while, then dish it out.

Now wash and dry the pan, heat up some more oil, and stir-fry the pork for about 2 minutes or until done, then pour it over on top of the cauliflower and serve.

Shredded pork with Szechuan-preserved vegetable

Szechuan-preserved vegetable is made of the root of a vegetable whose texture resembles a radish, pickled with chilli and salt. It is very hot and salty, so you only need a small amount.

½ lb (225 g) pork
2 oz (50 g) Szechuan-preserved vegetable
3–4 spring onions
1 teaspoon soya sauce
enough oil for shallow-frying

Choose a cut of pork that is not too lean, and shred it into strips the size of matchsticks. Wipe off the excess chilli on the surface of the preserved vegetable and shred it to the same size. Use the white part of the spring onions only, cut into short bits.

Heat up some oil in a pan, and before it gets too hot, throw in the pork, separating the strips by stirring vigorously. When the colour of the meat starts to change, put in about 1 teaspoon of soya sauce and the spring onions, continue stirring for a while, then add the preserved vegetable and cook all together for about 1 minute more, or until the pork and vegetable are well blended with each other.

If you find this dish to be too hot, then you can wash the vegetable in water before shredding, and add a little cornflour to the pork before frying. This way the meat will taste more tender and the vegetable less hot.

Meat slices with spring onions

This recipe originated in Shantung, a province in the North with which Peking cuisine is closely associated, famous for its leek- and onion-flavoured dishes. You can substitute either onions or leeks for spring onions, and use beef or lamb instead of pork; the method is the same.

½ lb (225 g) pork (or beef or lamb)
½ lb (225 g) spring onions (or onions or leeks)
¼ oz (7 g) Wooden Ears
1 tablespoon soya sauce
enough oil for shallow-frying
a little monosodium glutamate

Cut the meat into thin slices; cut the spring onions or leeks into 1-in (25-mm) lengths, or if using onions, slice them into small pieces. Soak the Wooden Ears in warm water for 20 minutes, discarding the hard stalks if any, and slice them too.

Heat up some oil in a pan until it smokes, quickly stir-fry the onions or leeks for about 1 minute (but with spring onions, only for a few seconds) add the meat and Wooden Ears with a little soya sauce and monosodium glutamate, keep the heat high and continue stirring for about 1½–2 minutes; then it is done.

Shredded pork with green peppers

The green pepper or pimento, a native of America, is now cultivated in all parts of the world. Its crunchy texture makes it very popular in China.

½ lb (225 g) pork
½ lb (225 g) green peppers
1 tablespoon soya sauce
1 tablespoon sherry
1 teaspoon sugar
enough oil for shallow-frying
a little salt

Wash the green peppers in cold water, slit them open and discard the seeds and stalks. Shred them and the pork into thin strips.

Heat up some oil in a pan, stir-fry the pork with soya sauce, sugar and sherry, and dish it out when the juice starts to bubble.

Now wash the pan and heat it up again. Pour in 2–3 tablespoons of oil, wait till it smokes, throw in the green peppers, stir, add salt, continue stirring, then add the meat and cook together for a little longer. Dish out as soon as the juice starts to bubble.

It goes without saying that you can replace the pork with beef, or chicken, or indeed instead of green peppers you can use almost any other kind of vegetable. Equally, you need not shred all the ingredients into thin strips—they could be slices of any shape or size you wish, only bear in mind that both the meat and the vegetable should *match* each other.

Stuffed green peppers

For this recipe, use small, thin-skinned green peppers if possible.

½ lb (225 g) green peppers
½ lb (225 g) minced pork
2 spring onions
1 slice ginger root
2 tablespoons soya sauce
1 tablespoon sherry
2–3 tablespoons oil
¼ pt (140 ml) stock or water
1 teaspoon sugar
a little cornflour
a little salt

Mix the minced pork with finely chopped spring onions and ginger root, together with a little salt and 1 tablespoon each of sherry and soya sauce.

Wash the peppers, cut them in half and remove the seeds. Stuff them with the pork mixture and sprinkle with a little cornflour.

Heat 2–3 tablespoons of oil in a flat frying-pan, put in the stuffed peppers, meat side down, and fry for 2 minutes, shaking the pan now and then gently to make sure the meat is not stuck to the bottom of the pan. Now add a little sugar and more soya sauce together with the stock or water, allow to simmer for 10–15 minutes, then carefully lift the peppers on to a dish, meat side up, and serve.

Stir-fried pork and mange-touts

The mange-tout, also known as snow pea or sugar pea, is a kind of pea of which the pod is eaten as well as the seeds. Its season is extremely short, usually lasting from spring to early summer, so if you are unable to obtain it, then substitute any other green vegetable such as french beans, cabbage or green peppers.

½ lb (225 g) lean pork
½ lb (225 g) mange-touts (or any other vegetable in season)
1½ tablespoons soya sauce
1½ tablespoons sherry
1½ teaspoons sugar
1½ teaspoons cornflour
enough oil for shallow-frying
a little stock or water (if required)
a little salt

Slice the pork into small pieces and mix it with the soya sauce, sherry, sugar and cornflour.

Wash the mange-touts in cold water. If the pods are picked as soon as they are formed, they will not be stringy and therefore need only be topped and tailed.

Heat some oil in a frying-pan until it smokes, stir-fry the pork for about 30 seconds or until its colour turns pale, then remove it.

Wash and dry the pan and heat up some more oil until it smokes, stir-fry the mange-touts (or other vegetable) with a little salt for about 30 seconds before mixing in the pork, adding a little stock or water if required. Fry meat and vegetable together for a few more seconds. When it is done, the meat should be tender and the vegetable crisp and fresh. Serve immediately.

West Lake beef soup

This is really a Cantonese recipe, but West Lake is a famous beauty spot in Eastern China. Do not ask me the reason for the name—I have not the faintest idea!

¼ lb (100 g) tender steak
1 egg
1 oz (25 g) fresh parsley
2½ tablespoons cornflour
1 tablespoon soya sauce
½ tablespoon sherry
1 teaspoon sugar
1 teaspoon salt
¼ teaspoon baking powder
2 pt (1·1 l) stock or water
3 tablespoons cold water
a little olive oil
a little pepper

Finely chop the steak into small pieces—but not quite as small as mince. Now mix the beef with ½ teaspoon each of salt and sugar, ¼ teaspoon of baking powder, ½ tablespoon each of soya sauce, sherry, and cornflour, and a little olive oil. Let it marinate for at least 30 minutes.

To make the soup (this is best done just before serving), bring the stock or water to the boil, pour in the beaten egg together with a little more salt, soya sauce, sugar and pepper, add the beef, bring it to the boil again, then thicken it with a cornflour paste made by mixing 2 tablespoons of cornflour with 3 of cold water, and stir. Add finely chopped parsley and serve.

Pork laurel (mu-hsu pork)

Some explanation is needed for the name of this dish. In China, we have a tree called *kuei;* according to my dictionary, *kuei* is called laurel in English, and it is a shrub rather than a tree; but the laurels we have in the garden of our London home never seem to flower at all, while the Chinese laurel is a large tree which produces bright yellow, fragrant flowers in the autumn. The pork in this recipe is cooked with eggs, which give a yellow colour to the dish—hence the name. But to add to the confusion, the Chinese name of this dish is mu-hsu pork, *mu-hsu* being the classical name for laurel (are you still with me?). So you might say that calling it pork laurel is taking a poetic licence!

  ¼ lb (100 g) pork
  3 eggs
  2 spring onions
  1 tablespoon soya sauce
  1 tablespoon sherry
  3 tablespoons oil
  a little stock or water
  a little salt

Choose a piece of pork that is not too lean (spare rib chops would be ideal), and cut it into shreds the size of matchsticks; cut up the spring onions into pieces the same length.

Heat up 2 tablespoons of oil in a pan, and while waiting for it to smoke, beat up the eggs. Pour these in and lightly scramble them; dish them out before they set too hard.

Now heat up a little more oil, fry the spring onion and pork shreds together for about 1 minute or until the colour of the pork changes, then add 1 tablespoon each of soya sauce and sherry, a little salt and the scrambled eggs together with a little stock or water; let all the ingredients blend well, and when the juice starts to bubble it is ready. Traditionally, this dish is used as a filling for thin pancakes (see p. 95).

Pork laurel Shantung style

This is a superior version of the earlier recipe. The crunchiness of bamboo shoots and Wooden Ears give it an added texture.

  ¼ lb (100 g) pork
  3 eggs

2 oz (50 g) bamboo shoots
¼ oz (7 g) Wooden Ears
2 spring onions
1 tablespoon soya sauce
1 tablespoon sherry
3 tablespoons oil
a little stock or water
a little salt
a little monosodium glutamate
a few drops sesame seed oil

Shred the pork into matchstick-sized segments; do the same with the spring onions, bamboo shoots and Wooden Ears, having soaked the latter in warm water for about 20 minutes.

Scramble the lightly beaten eggs in hot oil as described earlier, dishing them out before they set too hard. Heat up some more oil, stir-fry the spring onions and pork together for a short while, then add the bamboo shoots and Wooden Ears with soya sauce, sherry, monosodium glutamate and a little stock or water; bring the mixture to the boil before adding the scrambled eggs, then put in a few drops of sesame seed oil and blend all the ingredients well before serving.

A variation of this recipe is to use dried Tiger Lily (also called yellow flower) instead of bamboo shoots. The method of cooking is exactly the same, but of course the flavour and texture will be slightly altered.

Thin pancakes

1 lb (450 g) plain flour
9 fl oz (250 ml) boiling water
a little vegetable oil

Sift the flour into a mixing-bowl and slowly pour in the boiling water, mixed with 1 teaspoon of oil, and while stirring with a pair of chopsticks or a wooden spoon. Do not be tempted to add any more water than the amount given; otherwise it will get too wet and become messy. Knead the mixture into a firm dough, then divide it

into 3 equal portions. Now roll out each portion into a long
'sausage', and cut each sausage into 8 equal pieces; then, by using
the palm of your hand, press each piece into a flat pancake. Brush
one of the pancakes with a little oil, and place another one on top
to form a 'sandwich', so that you end up with 12 sandwiches. Now,
using a rolling-pin to flatten each sandwich into a 6-in (150-mm)
circle, roll gently on each side on a lightly floured surface.

To cook, place a frying-pan over a high heat, and when it is hot,
reduce the heat to moderate. Put one pancake sandwich at a time
into the ungreased pan, and turn it over when it starts to puff up
with bubbles. It is done when little brown spots appear on the
underside; remove it from the pan and, very gently, peel apart the
two layers and fold them up.

If the pancakes are not to be served as soon as they are cooked,
they can be warmed up, either in a steamer or in the oven, for 5–10
minutes.

V
More Meat than Vegetables

Spare ribs in sweet and sour
   sauce
Fricassée spare ribs
Bean curd à la maison
Twice-cooked pork
Fragrant pork
Braised five flowers pork
Braised brisket of beef
Braised beef with tomatoes

Beef in oyster sauce
Red-cooked pork shoulder
Soya pork
Red-cooked mutton
Chinese hot-pot
   See also:
Red-cooked beef (p. 27)
Lions' heads (pork meat balls)
   (p. 36)

During the four thousand years or so of known Chinese history, the Imperial capital had always been in the northern parts of the country—with the exception of a few brief periods: notably during the Sung dynasty, when it was at Hangchow (1127–1279), and the Ming dynasty, when it was at Nanking (1368–1402). The Chinese Emperor was supposed to be the Son of Heaven, and he lived a very much enclosed life inside the Imperial Court, which was known as the 'Great Within'; he was entirely isolated from the people of the nation. He seldom ventured out of the Forbidden City at all, and never visited the other parts of his vast Empire—except when he was driven out by foreign invasion or rebellion, which happened now and again during the course of history.

It was Emperor Ch'ien Lung (1735–95), one of the most distinguished 'cultured' Emperors of the Ch'ing (Manchu) dynasty, who broke the ancient tradition by making an extensive tour of Southern China. This was unprecedented and soon became a legend. One of the most popular stories told at the time was that Ch'ien Lung would often disguise himself as an ordinary citizen and go out without his entourage to mingle with the people in the street. Naturally, there were many surprises in store for him, but what he was most amazed by was the discovery of the simple but delicious food eaten by his subjects, as opposed to the rich and elaborately prepared feasts he was served all the year round at the court. When he returned to Peking, he ordered the Imperial cook to prepare for him the simple dishes he had enjoyed at the food shops in the streets; but alas, the simple dishes prepared in the Imperial kitchens no longer had that magical taste he had first experienced.

In a way we have all had similar surprises and disappointments in our own lives. How many times have we heard people complain that a certain wonderful wine they have discovered in the hot sun of the Mediterranean countries never tastes the same back home, and very often people remember certain foods they had in their childhood but somehow could never recapture the same experience again in different surroundings. I mentioned in the Introduction to this book the thrill and excitement of my first encounter with sweet and sour spare ribs in a Cantonese restaurant, but I have never tasted anything like it since; no matter how hard I have tried with a number of different recipes, the results were always the same—good enough for most people, but never with that *je ne sais quoi* of when you first come across something wonderful.

Spare ribs in sweet and sour sauce

It is pork spare ribs that you use for this recipe; the cut is sometimes known as American spare ribs in England, since the original English spare rib is a quite different cut.

1 lb (450 g) pork spare ribs
1 small green pepper
1 egg yolk
2 tablespoons plus ½ teaspoon sugar
2 tablespoons wine vinegar
enough oil for deep-frying
a little cornflour
a little plain flour
a little salt
a little pepper

If you do not possess a cleaver, then get your butcher to chop each spare rib in half for you. Marinate them in a little salt and pepper, ½ teaspoon of sugar, 1 egg yolk and a little cornflour for about 10 minutes, then coat each piece with dry flour and fry them in hottish oil until crisp and golden. Scoop them out with a perforated spoon, and heat up the oil to boiling, then fry the spare ribs once more—but not too long, just enough to darken the colour a little.

Pour out the excess oil from the pan, leaving about 1 teaspoon, slice the green pepper, fry it for a few seconds, then add 2 tablespoons each of sugar and wine vinegar together with a little cornflour for thickening; when it starts bubbling, blend in the spare ribs and serve immediately.

You will find this dish quite different from what you are normally served in a run-of-the-mill Chinese restaurant. When done properly, the sauce should be bright and translucent, not too sweet nor too sharp. To add a little more contrast to the colour, you can use half a green and half a red pepper.

Fricassée spare ribs

Strictly speaking, a fricassée is a French method of preparing chicken in a white sauce. But in England the term is applied to various kinds of stewing. In the traditional Chinese method, called *chu*, an earthenware pot is used, but I have found that a cast-iron casserole is even better, since this dish is cooked on top of the oven. You can use an ordinary saucepan if you like, but it must have a tightly fitting lid.

> 1½ lb (680 g) pork spare ribs
> 2–3 spring onions (or a small onion)
> 2 cloves garlic
> 2 tablespoons black or yellow bean sauce
> 1 tablespoon sherry
> 1 tablespoon soya sauce
> 1 teaspoon sugar
> 1 teaspoon cornflour
> 2–3 tablespoons oil
> ¼ pt (140 ml) stock or water

Cut each individual rib into half, or ask your butcher to chop them up for you. (If this fails, with this recipe you can cook them whole, only they will take longer and also look rather clumsy when serving.) Marinate the pieces with 1 teaspoon each of sugar and cornflour, and 1 tablespoon each of sherry and soya sauce.

Now finely chop the garlic and cut the spring onions into 1-in (25-mm) lengths. Fry the spare ribs in a little hot oil for a short while—about ½ minute or so, then scoop them out with a perforated spoon. Next fry the chopped garlic and spring onions in the same pan with 2 tablespoons of black or yellow bean sauce, and at the same time blend in the spare ribs, stirring constantly to make sure all the pieces are well covered with the sauce. Now add a little stock or water and put the lid on tightly. What you have to do here is to listen carefully for the sizzling noise: does it sound too rapid, so that the heat has to be reduced? Or does it sound too weak, and therefore either you have put too much water in, or perhaps the heat has to be increased? All this is very important if you want to make this dish perfectly. Anyway, you have to open the lid now and again (not too often, say every 4–5 minutes) and add more water or stock until about ¼ pt (140 ml) in all is almost completely absorbed. This should take about 10–15 minutes, and then it will be ready for serving.

This dish should have a wonderful aroma, and the meat should not come off the bone too easily, but be very succulent.

One of the simple dishes Emperor Ch'ien Lung discovered among the common people was bean curd. This custard-like preparation of puréed and pressed soya beans is exceptionally high in protein, and is known in China as 'poor man's meat'. It is widely used in everyday home cooking and is most useful in absorbing and harmonizing the flavour of other ingredients. It is sold in cakes about 3 in (75 mm) square and 1 in (25 mm) thick in Oriental provision stores, and will keep fresh for several days if stored in water in the refrigerator. It has a rather unusual texture, and is an acquired taste which may not appeal to everybody immediately.

There is an almost endless variety of dishes in which bean curd can be used. The dish that Emperor Ch'ien Lung supposedly liked best is known as 'bean curd for family meals'. You could say it is a sort of chop suey, for it is a bean curd-based dish with bits of meat and fish or any left-overs thrown in. The best recipe I have come across is probably this one from Szechuan:

Bean curd à la maison

4 cakes bean curd
2 oz (50 g) pork

2 spring onions
2 tablespoons soya sauce
1 teaspoon chilli purée (optional)
½ teaspoon cornflour
½ pt (280 ml) stock or water
enough oil for shallow-frying
a little salt

Slice each square of bean curd into ¼-in (6-mm) thick slices, then cut each slice into 4 or 6 pieces. Cut the pork into thin slices and the spring onions into ½-in (12-mm) lengths.

Shallow-fry the bean curd pieces in a little oil on both sides until they turn light golden, gently scoop them out with a fish slice and put them aside. Now heat up some more oil and stir-fry the pork (with 1 teaspoon of chilli purée if so desired) for a few seconds, then add a little less than ½ pt (280 ml) of stock or water mixed with 2 tablespoons of soya sauce, together with the bean curd; bring to the boil, then reduce the heat and let it bubble for 2–3 minutes; now add the spring onions and a little salt, continue cooking for 1 minute, then mix ½ teaspoon of cornflour with a little water and pour it all over the contents just before serving.

Of course, you can replace the pork with almost any meat you like, or indeed you can use more than one variety at the same time— it all depends on what you have readily available: prawns, cooked ham, small bits of left-overs from your Sunday joint, etc. To make it more colourful, a little green vegetable will be an excellent addition. Just use your own initiative and be experimental.

Twice-cooked pork

Among the cheapest cuts of meat on the market is belly pork (called bacon piece in the USA); in China it is known as 'five flowers meat' because when viewed in cross-section, the alternate layers of fat and meat form a pretty pink and white pattern.

1 lb (450 g) belly pork
2 oz (50 g) bamboo shoots
2–3 spring onions

2 tablespoons black or yellow bean sauce
1 tablespoon soya sauce
1 tablespoon sherry
1 teaspoon sugar
1 teaspoon chilli purée (optional)
enough oil for shallow-frying

Place the piece of pork whole in a saucepan and cover it with water, bring it to the boil and let it simmer for about 40 minutes. Meanwhile, cut the bamboo shoots into slices and the spring onions into ½-in (12-mm) lengths.

Skin the pork, and if you are calorie-conscious, cut off some of the excess fat. Slice the meat into thin pieces half the size of a matchbox or even smaller. Keep the water for stock.

Heat up a small amount of oil in a frying-pan, throw in the spring onions followed by 2 tablespoons of soya bean paste, stir for a couple of seconds, then put in the pork and bamboo shoot slices, add 1 tablespoon each of sherry and soya sauce, 1 teaspoon of sugar and a little stock from the pork, continue stirring for about 1½ minutes, and then it is ready. For those who like hot food, a teaspoon of chilli purée added at the last minute will give this delicious dish an extra-piquant taste, as preferred in Szechuan where it originated.

You can omit the bamboo shoots or substitute any other seasonal vegetable, in which case stir-fry the fresh vegetable first for a few seconds before adding the pork to the pan.

Fragrant pork

Another way of cooking the cheap cut of belly pork. If you cook it in a fairly large quantity, it could be served for a number of meals or be used in other dishes such as Yangchow fried rice (p. 80), stir-fried ten varieties (p. 79) or bean curd à la maison (p. 102).

2 lb (900 g) belly pork
1 spring onion
1 slice ginger root
4 tablespoons soya sauce
4 tablespoons sherry

1 tablespoon sugar
1 teaspoon Five Spice powder
1 teaspoon salt
lettuce or cabbage leaves for garnish

If you bought the pork in one or two big pieces, cut it into large chunks about 6 in × 3 in (150 mm × 75 mm). Place it in a large saucepan with the spring onion, ginger root, salt, Five Spice powder, sherry, soya sauce, sugar, and just enough water to cover the pork. Now bring it to the boil, and keep the heat fairly high for about 3 hours, adding a little water now and again to keep it from drying out, but otherwise keeping the lid firmly closed so that the meat juices do not seep out.

To serve, remove the meat from the sauce, cut it into thin slices rather like bacon, and serve it on a bed of lettuce leaves or cooked cabbage. The sauce can be stored and re-used for cooking other meat or chicken, or the egg dish on p. 75.

Braised five flowers pork

This is the most popular way of cooking pork in China. Again, if you cook more than you need for one meal, the rest can be warmed up and served again, or used as an ingredient for a number of recipes.

1½ lb (680 g) belly pork
2 spring onions
1 slice ginger root
4 tablespoons soya sauce
4 tablespoons sherry
1 tablespoon sugar
½ teaspoon Five Spice powder
a little oil
some vegetables (optional)

Cut the pork into 1-in (25-mm) cubes, the spring onions into ½-in (12-mm) lengths, and the ginger root into 2 or 3 small pieces.

In a warm, greased pan, brown the pork lightly, then add the spring onions, sherry, soya sauce, sugar and Five Spice powder with enough water to cover the meat. Bring it to the boil and skim the surface; now place a tightly fitting lid on the pan, reduce the heat, and let it simmer gently for 1½ hours.

You can serve it on its own or add in the last 30 minutes of cooking some vegetables such as cabbage, carrots, turnips, bamboo shoots or bean curd, all of which will help to absorb the fat from the meat as well as improve the flavour.

Braised brisket of beef

As I mentioned earlier, beef is regarded as inferior to pork in China, so brisket of beef is about the lowest of the low! However, if you follow this recipe, you will end up with a nourishing, delicious and economical dish.

    1½ lb (680 g) brisket of beef (or shin shank)
    3 spring onions
    4 slices ginger root
    3–4 tablespoons soya sauce
    2 tablespoons sherry
    1 tablespoon sugar
    ¼ teaspoon Five Spice powder
    a little oil

Trim the beef of excess fat, but do not overdo this as the fat helps to enrich the juice and keep the meat tender. Cut the beef into 1-in (25-mm) squares, or longer chunks of the same width.

Bring to the boil 1½ pt (850 ml) of water and boil the beef chunks rapidly for 3 minutes. Now turn off the heat (if you cook by electricity then remove the saucepan from the cooker), and scoop out the beef with a perforated spoon.

Put 1 tablespoon of sugar in the water, and after about 10 minutes, all the impurities will sink to the bottom of the pan, leaving the stock clear. Drain it through a fine sieve and keep it aside.

Heat up a small amount of oil in a frying-pan, and stir-fry the finely chopped spring onion and ginger root, followed by the parboiled beef with the soya sauce, sherry and Five Spice powder. Stir for a few minutes, then transfer it back to the saucepan and add the stock. Bring it to the boil, put on the lid, turn down the heat, and let it simmer gently for 2 or 3 hours; by then the juice should be reduced to less than ½ pt (280 ml) and have become a rich, brown sauce with a wonderful aroma.

You can either serve it immediately, in which case skim off the excess fat, or let it cool and then de-fat and reheat it the next day.

Any cheap cuts of mutton (such as breast or stewing mutton) can be cooked in the same way, but perhaps increasing the amount of spring onions and ginger root.

Braised beef with tomatoes

Another way of cooking the cheaper cuts of beef is this recipe from Tientsin in Northern China. As you can see from the list of ingredients below, nothing out of the ordinary is required in its preparation, and therefore it should appeal to almost everybody.

1½ lb (680 g) stewing or braising beef
1 lb (450 g) tomatoes
2 spring onions
2 cloves garlic
2 slices ginger root (optional)
3 oz (75 g) sugar
2 tablespoons soya sauce
2 tablespoons sherry
a little oil
a little cornflour
a little pepper

Place the beef, cut into large pieces, in a saucepan and cover it with cold water, add a spring onion and a clove of garlic (also a slice of ginger root if you like, but this is not important), bring it to the boil and simmer gently with a tightly fitting lid for about 2 hours. Add more water freely during the course of cooking.

Skin the tomatoes by plunging them in boiling water for a short while, then cut them into small pieces and stew them with 2 oz (50 g) of sugar in another saucepan until they become almost a purée-like liquid.

Scoop out the beef when it is done and let it cool a little, then cut it into small squares and fry it in hot oil for a few seconds. Leave a little oil in the pan and throw in 1 crushed clove of garlic, let it turn golden, then add 1 finely chopped spring onion, 1 slice of ginger root (optional), the sherry and soya sauce, a little sugar and about ½ pt (280 ml) stock from the meat. Blend well, add the beef and bring it to the boil, then reduce the heat and cook gently for 5 minutes. Drain off any excess juice, add the tomatoes and cook a further 2–3 minutes. Just before serving, thicken the gravy by mixing in a little cornflour and sprinkle the dish with freshly ground pepper.

You will find this dish a pleasant change from plain stewed beef, and well worth the extra effort. Needless to say, any left-overs can be reheated and will taste just as good the next day.

Beef in oyster sauce

The Chinese are fond of combining sharply contrasted flavours in a way that would seem highly unusual to a Westerner—another example of this is the dish of kidneys and prawns cooked together (p. 121). One of the most successful combinations is this famous Cantonese dish of beef cooked in oyster sauce.

Oyster sauce is by no means a luxury in China, since in fact it is only soya sauce with oyster flavouring. It should cost not much more than the best soya sauce, and a small bottle will go a long way as you only need a little at a time.

½ lb (280 g) frying steak
2 tablespoons oyster sauce
2 spring onions
1 slice ginger root
2–3 tablespoons oil
a little sherry
a little cornflour
a little salt

Cut the beef into thin slices across the grain, mix with the oyster sauce, a little salt, sherry and cornflour and marinate for about 1 hour. Cut the spring onions into 1-in (25-mm) lengths and chop up the ginger root.

Heat up a pan and let it get really hot before pouring in 2–3 table-spoons of oil, wait for it to bubble, then throw in the spring onions and ginger root and give them a stir or two; now add the beef and stir vigorously for at most 10 seconds; unless you like your steak overdone, dish it out quickly. Another thing to watch here is the heat which must be as high as you can manage all the time.

Red-cooked pork shoulder

This is a famous dish from Southern China, a must for any festivities big or small; I suppose it is the nearest equivalent to a traditional Sunday joint in Britain.

1 pork shoulder (3½–4 lb, 1·6–1·8 kg)
6 spring onions
6 tablespoons soya sauce
3 tablespoons sherry
3 tablespoons crystallized (or brown) sugar
½ teaspoon Five Spice powder
some vegetables (optional)

Pork shoulder sometimes is known as hand of pork in England and picnic shoulder in the USA (a more expensive cut is the leg part known as knuckle in England or ham in the USA). It is usually sold with the bone in and the rind on.

Before cooking, blanch it by placing the whole piece of pork in cold water and bringing it to the boil for a few minutes, then discard the water and wash the pork under the cold tap.

Now place the meat in a large pot, add the spring onions, soya sauce, sherry, crystallized sugar (brown sugar will do), Five Spice powder and 1 pt (570 ml) of cold water. Cover it with a tightly fitting lid and bring it to the boil over high heat, then reduce the heat and let it simmer gently for 2–3 hours, turning it over carefully several times during cooking. There should be very little liquid left at the end; if necessary, turn up the heat and cook uncovered until the liquid is reduced and has become rather thick.

Traditionally, the pork is served whole in a large bowl with the juice poured over it. Sometimes root vegetables such as carrots or bamboo shoots are added during the last 30 minutes of cooking in order to absorb some of the fat. When it is done perfectly, the rind and meat should be soft enough to be pulled off the bone with a pair of chopsticks or a fork. Any left-overs can be cut into slices and served cold.

Soya pork

This is a famous Shanghai recipe, traditionally served cold, and is an ideal dish to accompany wine.

    1 lb (450 g) belly pork (in one piece if possible)
    2 spring onions
    2 slices ginger root
    3 tablespoons soya sauce
    3 tablespoons sherry
    3 tablespoons crystallized (or brown) sugar
    $\frac{1}{4}$ teaspoon Five Spice powder
    a little red colouring (Chinese 'red powder' or cochineal)
    a little salt
    lettuce leaves for garnish

Wash and wipe dry the pork, rub all sides with salt then leave it to marinate for at least 2 hours.

Next place the pork in 1 pt (570 ml) of water in a deep saucepan together with the spring onions, ginger root, Five Spice powder and a little 'red powder' (if you can get it from a Chinese provision store—failing that, use a few drops of cochineal). Bring it to the boil, then reduce the heat and add the soya sauce, sherry, and crystallized sugar. Simmer with the lid on for about 2 hours, turning the pork now and again; by then the sauce should have been reduced to almost nothing. Now remove the pan from the heat and let the pork cool before slicing it into small pieces, arrange them neatly on a bed of lettuce leaves and pour whatever is left of the sauce on top before serving.

Red-cooked mutton

This is a very simple way of cooking the cheaper cuts of mutton and lamb—or indeed any other type of meat, such as pork or beef. It can be cooked the day before you need it and warmed up and served whenever you require.

1½ lb (680 g) mutton or stewing lamb
1 clove garlic
2 slices ginger root
2–3 tablespoons soya sauce
2–3 tablespoons sherry
¼ teaspoon Five Spice powder
a little sugar
a little stock or water

First wash the meat in cold water thoroughly, then dip it in boiling water for a short while before cutting it into small squares. Now place the meat pieces in a saucepan and add sherry, ginger root and Five Spice powder together with stock or water, bring it to the boil, then reduce the heat and simmer for about 1 hour. Now add the soya sauce, a little sugar, and crushed clove of garlic, cook for a further 30 minutes or until almost no juice is left, and then it is ready.

Chinese hot-pot

Now for something completely different, here is an unusual way of serving Chinese food: for once, the actual cooking is done not in the kitchen but on the dining-table, and is very much a do-it-yourself affair.

You can get a charcoal-burning hot-pot from most Chinese stores. It may seem to be a large outlay, and for years my wife and I had doubts about its usefulness before eventually buying one; but I can assure you that it is a sound investment, besides looking most attractive and impressive on the table. There is nothing more warming on a cold winter's day than to catch a drift of burning charcoal and see the steaming pot bubbling with its delicious contents. It never fails to delight our guests, and our children always claim that it is the most fun way of serving a meal.

Also known as Mongolian fire pot, this dish is not unlike a fondue; stock or plain water is brought to the boil over a charcoal burner on the centre of the table and everybody cooks his or her own meat in it. There is no strict rule as to what ingredients you must or must not use, they vary enormously from place to place or according to seasonal availability; but it is definitely a winter dish, therefore much more popular in Northern China. It is not just a warming but also a most exciting way of eating, particularly with children.

The quantity I have given should be enough for at least six to ten people. This is a complete meal on its own; I do not think you will need anything else to go with it.

1 lb (450 g) lamb fillet (or pork or beef, or all three)
½ lb (225 g) chicken breast
½ lb (225 g) prawns (or fish fillet, or both)
½ lb (225 g) liver (chicken or pork)
½ lb (225 g) kidney (pork or lamb)
1 oz (25 g) Chinese dried mushrooms (or ½ lb, 225 g, fresh mushrooms)
1 lb (450 g) Chinese cabbage (or spinach)
2–3 cakes bean curd (optional)
stock or water to fill the pot

For the dip:
3–4 tablespoons soya sauce
a little sugar
2–3 spring onions
2–3 slices ginger root

Cut the meats into as thin slices as you possibly can; arrange them either separately on a large plate or in small individual dishes. Soak the dried mushrooms in warm water for ½ hour or so, then discard the stalks and cut the mushrooms also into thin slices. Wash the cabbage or spinach and cut it into small pieces. Cut the bean curd into small pieces—bamboo shoots, carrots or any other vegetables can be substituted here—and arrange them all neatly, either together or separately, like the meats.

Finely chop the spring onions and ginger root, mix them with the soya sauce and a little sugar, put this mixture in two or three little sauce dishes and place these on the table within easy reach of everyone.

All these preparations should be done beforehand. Now first cook some of the vegetables in the stock or water on the table; after it has simmered for a few minutes each person picks up a piece of meat of his or her choice with chopsticks (or a fork) and dips it in the boiling soup for a very short time—usually as soon as the colour of the meat changes it is done—then quickly retrieves it and dips it in sauce and eats it while still piping hot.

When all the meats have been eaten, add the remaining vegetables to the pot, let it boil vigorously for a few minutes, then ladle out the contents into individual bowls and serve as a most delicious soup.

VI
'Let a Hundred Flowers Bloom'
—Kidneys and Liver

Stir-fried kidney flowers
Kidney flowers with celery
Kidney flowers Szechuan style
Stir-fried prawns and kidneys
'Agitated' kidney flowers

Stir-fried liver flowers
Pig's liver with Wooden Ears
Fried liver Szechuan style   ·
Calf's liver Canton style

A Chinese housewife who sets out to do her daily shopping each morning seldom has a preconceived idea as to what sort of food she will be buying, for much depends on what she will find when she gets to the market. Her prime consideration will be the quality and freshness of the food—and also the value for money. As a small child, I used to accompany my nanny to the market every morning on my way to kindergarten. To get the best and freshest meat and vegetables, you had to be really early, for by mid-morning there would be hardly anything to choose from except a few pathetic-looking left-overs.

I used to enjoy these shopping expeditions enormously. I would help my nanny to pick and choose, and sometimes even bargained for her, to the great amusement of the vendors and storekeepers. My wife thinks that is probably why I have such an eye for bargains when we go out shopping together.

A market-place in China was a bustling and noisy place. Besides the permanent stores, there were dozens of makeshift stands where the peasants from the outskirts of the town would bring in their farm produce to sell—the chickens and ducks were always alive and kicking, and the fish swimming in water; all the vegetables were so fresh that you could still see morning dew on them, since they were truly dawn-picked only a few hours earlier. I learned from my nanny how to distinguish the freshly picked vegetables from ones that had been picked the day before and had been artificially kept fresh by soaking in water all night.

Years later, when my parents lived in Oxford, there used to be a covered market in the centre of the city, not unlike the one I knew in China, but there was no early morning rush, no live poultry or fish, nor any vegetables that one would really call fresh. Later still, on the Continent, I came across several markets which recaptured a little of the Chinese atmosphere, but alas, one's childhood memories linger on!

In this chapter, I shall offer a selection of slightly unusual dishes using ingredients which, though easily obtainable, may have been ignored by cooks who are not sure how best to deal with them. Do not, however, be disappointed when you discover that there are no recipes for such exotic items as bird's nest soup or shark's fins; these are very expensive to buy and tedious to prepare, and besides they are definitely not everyday, homely food, so there is no room for them in this book.

I have already mentioned the use of giblets (p. 78), but not the wide use of offal or variety meats in Chinese cooking. Nothing edible is thrown away in China. In the case of pork, not only the kidneys, liver, brains, trotters and head are considered as delicacies, but also all the entrails, and the blood, are very much used. Because of their reputedly extra nutritive value, some butchers in certain parts of China would charge for items such as kidneys and liver *more* than the best 'ordinary' cuts of meat. On the other hand, in the part of the country we lived in during the war with Japan, the butchers had to force the customers to take some offal as a make-weight with their purchases of meat.

Stir-fried kidney flowers

If ever I were a castaway on a desert island, the one non-fish dish I should miss most would undoubtedly be this. Kidney dishes have always been among my favourites, and this one is my favourite of all. The recipe comes from Shantung; for years it used to be on the menu in a Chinese restaurant in Paris, but the last time I went there with my family, to our great disappointment, the restaurant had changed hands, and our favourite dish was no longer served there.

½ lb (225 g) pork kidney
2 oz (50 g) water chestnuts
2 oz (50 g) bamboo shoots
¼ oz (7 g) Wooden Ears
¼ lb (100 g) seasonal green vegetable (lettuce, cabbage or spinach)
1 spring onion

1 clove garlic
1 slice ginger root
1 tablespoon soya sauce
1 tablespoon wine vinegar
enough oil for shallow-frying
a little cornflour
a little salt

The colour of pork kidneys should be bright reddish brown; do not buy any that have turned dark purple, or if they do not smell fresh. First peel off the thin white skin covering the kidneys if the butcher has not already done so, then split them in half lengthways and discard the fat and white, tough parts in the middle. Score the surface of the kidneys diagonally in a criss-cross pattern and then cut them into medium-sized pieces, so that when cooked they will open up and resemble ears of corn—hence the name of this dish.

Slice the water chestnuts and bamboo shoots; soak the Wooden Ears in warm water for about 20 minutes and discard the hard parts; blanch the green vegetables; finely chop the spring onion, ginger root and garlic.

Heat up some oil in a pan until it smokes, fry the kidneys for a very short while, stirring all the time to make sure all the pieces are separated, then quickly scoop them out with a perforated spoon, and pour out the excess oil, leaving about 2 tablespoons in the pan. Now fry the spring onion, ginger root and garlic, followed by the water chestnuts, bamboo shoots, Wooden Ears and green vegetables, add the vinegar and salt, stir a few more times before putting in the kidneys, add the soya sauce and a little cornflour mixed to a paste with stock or water, let all the ingredients blend well, and serve.

This dish should have a harmonious balance of aroma, texture and colour and is ideal for accompanying wine, even though it has a touch of vinegar in it.

Kidney flowers with celery

This is a Cantonese recipe and is slightly easier to prepare than the previous one.

½ lb (225 g) pork kidney
1 medium-sized head celery
3–4 spring onions
4 slices ginger root
1 clove garlic
1 tablespoon soya sauce
1 tablespoon sherry
1 teaspoon sugar
enough oil for shallow-frying
a little cornflour
a little stock or water
a little salt
a little pepper
a few drops sesame seed oil (optional)

Prepare the kidneys as described in the previous recipe. Marinate them in the soya sauce and sherry together with a little ground pepper. Wash the celery well and cut it diagonally, giving it half a turn between each cut so that the pieces are diamond-shaped. Cut the spring onions into 1-in (25-mm) lengths and finely chop the garlic. Make a thin paste by mixing 1 teaspoon of sugar and a little cornflour with stock or water.

First stir-fry the celery with a little salt in hot oil, and put it aside. Now heat up some more oil and throw in the garlic, ginger root slices and spring onions, followed by the kidney; stir for a little while, then add the celery. Blend them well before adding the paste mixture, and bring it to the boil. If desired, a few drops of sesame seed oil may be added before serving.

Kidney flowers Szechuan style

This is a hot and sour version of kidney flowers, as its origin suggests. Both the bamboo shoots and dried mushrooms called for in this recipe can be substituted, as the main character of the recipe comes from the piquant sauce rather than the supplementary ingredients used.

½ lb (225 g) pork kidney
2 oz (50 g) bamboo shoots (or carrots, celery, courgettes, etc)
¼ oz (7 g) Chinese dried mushrooms (or ¼ lb, 100 g, fresh mushrooms)
3–4 small dried red chillis
enough oil for shallow-frying
a little sherry
a little cornflour

For the sauce:
2 spring onions
1 clove garlic
2 slices ginger root
1 tablespoon soya sauce
1 tablespoon vinegar
1 tablespoon sugar
½ tablespoon chilli sauce
a little cornflour
a little pepper
a little monosodium glutamate

Prepare the kidneys as for the previous recipes and marinate the pieces with a little salt, pepper, sherry and cornflour. Cut the bamboo shoots and mushrooms (or their substitutes) into slices. Finely chop the spring onions, ginger root, and garlic and mix them with the other ingredients of the sauce.

First fry the kidneys for a very short while in hot oil, then scoop them out with a perforated spoon and stir-fry the vegetables with the hot and sour sauce; replace the kidneys and when everything is well blended it is ready.

This is a most piquant and delicious dish, but no ordinary table wine is strong enough to go with it—not even sherry—so in China we accompany it with a strong spirit. This may sound masochistic to you, but try it with brandy or whisky—it is sensational!

Stir-fried prawns and kidneys

Having given you recipes for kidneys from the North (Shantung),

South (Canton), and West (Szechuan), now it is the turn of Eastern China, in this case Shanghai. You may think the idea of combining prawns and kidneys is rather strange, but the Chinese believe this technique of mixing two entirely different ingredients helps to promote an exchange of flavours, each acquiring a new flavour at the same time, and acting as a seasoning agent on the other. It is a matter of 'give and take', rather as in a well-matched marriage—though one must not get too philosophical about it. Another example of an unusual blend is beef in oyster sauce (p. 108).

¼ lb (100 g) peeled prawns or shrimps
½ lb (225 g) pork kidneys
2 oz (50 g) bamboo shoots (or celery, carrots, etc)
½ oz (15 g) Chinese dried mushrooms (or ¼ lb, 100 g, fresh mushrooms)
a small amount of seasonal green vegetable (lettuce, cabbage, spinach, etc)
1–2 spring onions
1 egg white
1 tablespoon soya sauce
1 tablespoon sherry
1 tablespoon sugar
enough oil for shallow-frying
a little stock or water
a little cornflour
a little salt
a few drops sesame seed oil

Wash and dry the peeled prawns, mix in a little salt, the white of an egg, and cornflour, and leave them to marinate in the refrigerator for about 2 hours. Prepare the kidneys as for previous recipes, and mix in a little salt and cornflour. Cut the vegetables into slices, but keep the spring onions separate.

Heat up a large pan, warm up some oil, and quickly stir-fry the prawns for a very short while, followed by the kidneys. Stir to separate the pieces, then scoop them all out with a perforated spoon.

Heat up the remains of the oil and stir-fry the spring onions first, then all the other vegetables with a little salt; now add the soya sauce, sherry and sugar and some stock or water, and bring this to the boil before blending in the prawns and kidneys together with a little cornflour paste. Continue stirring a few more times and add a dash of sesame seed oil just before serving.

'Agitated' kidney flowers

Another simple-to-prepare dish from Peking, which when served side by side with 'agitated' prawns (p. 143) gives an interesting contrast in texture and colour.

Readers must forgive me for introducing this rather unusual cooking method called 'agitating'. The Chinese term is *ts'ang*, which is hard to define; it can be loosely translated as 'to excite', and involves marinating the main ingredient with highly flavoured seasonings such as vinegar, wine and ginger root. But I thought if you served 'excited kidneys' to your guests, they might get the wrong idea, so I have used the term 'agitated' instead.

$\frac{1}{2}$ lb (225 g) pork kidney
1 tablespoon sherry
a few thin slices ginger root
a little salt
a little monosodium glutamate
a few drops sesame seed oil

Clean and prepare the kidneys as in the previous recipes, scoring the surface diagonally in a criss-cross pattern before cutting them into thin slices. Cook them in boiling water for about 3 minutes, then drain and run cold water over them for a few seconds before dishing them out.

Now place a few thinly slivered ginger root slices on the kidney slices, then mix the sherry, salt, monosodium glutamate and sesame seed oil, pour it over the dish and leave to marinate for a while before serving.

Stir-fried liver flowers

Pig's liver is held in high regard in China for its nutritive value.

When it is done in this quick stir-fried way, even young children who normally dislike 'liver and bacon' would relish it.

½ lb (225 g) pig's liver
2 oz (50 g) bamboo shoots (or celery, courgettes, etc)
¼ oz (7 g) Chinese dried mushrooms (or ¼ lb, 100 g, fresh mushrooms)
2 spring onions
at least 5 tablespoons oil
a little soya sauce
a little cornflour
a little salt

Soak the dried mushrooms in warm water for about 30 minutes, discard any hard stalks, slice them if they are large, but leave them whole if small. Slice the bamboo shoots finely and cut the spring onions into ½-in (12-mm) lengths. Wash the liver, discard the white bits and slice it into triangular pieces, but not too thin—about ⅛ in (3 mm) thick.

Heat up a little oil in a pan and stir-fry the spring onions, bamboo shoots and mushrooms with a little salt for a short while. Dish them out and put them aside.

Now heat some more oil in the pan—quite a lot, at least 3–4 tablespoons; while waiting for it to smoke, which will take a few minutes, quickly pour some boiling water to cover the slices of liver in a mixing-bowl, stir with a pair of chopsticks or a fork, strain away the water and mix a little cornflour and soya sauce with the liver, then fry it in the hot oil; stir round 4–5 times before blending in the partly cooked mushrooms and bamboo shoots, stir a few times more and then it is ready to serve. The crucial point here is timing, but provided you keep cool during the whole operation it is comparatively simple. Another thing to remember is you must use a large amount of oil; if you find the dish rather greasy, then strain off the excess oil before serving.

Pig's liver with Wooden Ears

This is the most popular way of serving pig's liver in China. The contrast between the crunchiness of the Wooden Ears and the tender smoothness of the liver makes it extremely palatable.

½ lb (225 g) pig's liver
½ oz (15 g) Wooden Ears
2 spring onions
at least 6 tablespoons oil
2 tablespoons soya sauce
½ tablespoon cornflour
a little salt

Soak the Wooden Ears in warm water for about 20 minutes; tear the large ones into smaller pieces and discard any hard stalks. Cut the spring onions into ½-in (12-mm) lengths. Wash the liver, discard the white membranes and, just before cooking, cut it into medium slices about ⅛ in (3 mm) thick.

Heat up a little oil in a pan and throw in the spring onions, followed by the Wooden Ears; stir, add a little salt, stir a few more times and then dish it out.

Next heat up some more oil (about 4–5 tablespoons). While waiting for it to smoke, quickly pour some boiling water over the liver in a large bowl, stir to separate each piece, then drain away the water and mix the liver with the soya sauce and cornflour. Now fry the liver in hot oil, stir 4–5 times before adding the partly cooked Wooden Ears; stir together 3–4 times more, and then it is ready. Again strain off any excess oil before serving.

Fried liver Szechuan style

This is a slightly simpler way of cooking liver. As with most Szechuan dishes, the emphasis is on the piquant sauce, and you can substitute the vegetable quite freely, replacing bamboo shoots with any other that has a crunchy texture: Wooden Ears, celery, green peppers, etc.

1 lb (450 g) pig's liver
2 oz (50 g) bamboo shoots (or other vegetable, or ½ oz, 15 g,
  Wooden Ears)

1–2 spring onions
2–3 slices ginger root
enough oil for shallow-frying
a little sherry
a little salt
a little pepper
a few drops sesame seed oil

For the sauce:
1 clove garlic
1 tablespoon soya sauce
1 tablespoon sherry
2 tablespoons sugar
a little monosodium glutamate
a little cornflour

Clean and slice the liver, then mix in a little salt, freshly ground pepper, sherry and cornflour.

Slice the bamboo shoots or other vegetables and finely chop the spring onions and ginger root. Prepare the sauce by mixing the sugar, sherry, soya sauce, monosodium glutamate and finely chopped garlic together with a little cornflour and water solution.

Heat up some oil in a pan until it smokes and stir-fry the liver for a few seconds, then quickly scoop it out with a perforated spoon. Next fry the spring onions and ginger root with the bamboo shoots or other vegetables; after a few stirs add the partly cooked liver together with the ready-mixed sauce, and when all the ingredients are well blended it is done. Just before serving, add a few drops of sesame seed oil and more freshly ground pepper. The dish should have a lovely fragrance and texture.

Calf's liver Canton style

This delicious Cantonese dish also has the fuller name of 'braised calf's liver with ginger and onions', and it is quite easy to cook. If you find calf's liver too expensive or difficult to obtain, then by all means use ox liver instead.

¾ lb (340 g) calf's (or ox) liver
1 large onion
4 spring onions
6 slices ginger root
2 cloves garlic
a little soya sauce
1 tablespoon oyster sauce
a little sherry
enough oil for shallow-frying
a little cornflour
a little stock or water
a little sugar
a little salt
a little pepper

Clean and slice the liver and mix in a little salt, pepper, sugar, soya sauce, sherry and cornflour; let it marinate for about 30 minutes.

Slice the onion, cut the spring onions into ½-in (12-mm) lengths, shred the ginger root and crush the garlic. Prepare the sauce by mixing 1 tablespoon each of soya sauce and oyster sauce with a little sugar, cornflour and stock or water.

Heat up some oil in a pan, and while waiting for it to smoke, quickly pour some boiling water to cover the liver, drain and fry it in the hot oil for a very short while.

Now fry the onion, garlic and ginger root, followed by the liver, add a little more sherry and place a lid over the pan for a few seconds. Blend in the ready-mixed sauce and spring onions, bring it back to the boil and it is ready.

Even though this dish has a strong onion and ginger flavour, it is an ideal accompaniment to wine. I should choose a full-bodied wine such as Châteauneuf-du-Pape or Hermitage (either red or white), or otherwise stick to sherry.

VII
Fish without Chips

Braised fish steak
Fried fish fingers
Fried fish slices
Red-cooked carp
Carp with sweet and sour sauce
Braised perch à la maison
Crab with spring onions and
  ginger
Fu yung crab
Fried prawns
Phoenix tail prawns
'Agitated' prawns
Prawn balls assembly

Prawns in shells
Sesame seed prawn toast
Fish slices and mushrooms
  assembly
'Smoked' fish
Sweet and sour fish
Fish head soup
    See also:
Stir-fried prawns and peas (p.
  39)
Stir-fried prawns and kidneys
  (p. 121)

E

In China, fish is far more widely eaten as food than meat, partly because of its abundance, which makes it comparatively less expensive. This tendency is not confined only to the regions along the coastline, but in all other parts inland, where there are plenty of freshwater fish from rivers, lakes and ponds—in the countryside, ponds are not just used as reservoirs for agriculture, but for extensive fish farming as well.

I was rather puzzled when I first came to England and observed that although surrounded by sea, the British treated fish with distrust. However, soon I discovered the explanation—this was in the days before ready-prepared frozen fish was widely available on the market. An average housewife who sets out shopping is confronted with a vast variety of species, some glowering at her with strangely shaped heads, and is alarmed and confused. Added to this is the factor that most people have childhood memories of poorly prepared fish dishes that have left (literally) a bad taste.

Nowadays, the old-fashioned type of fishmonger's is disappearing fast to make way for streamlined supermarkets, where one can usually find a fresh fish counter alongside the frozen packets, so the choice is wide. The fishmonger—old or new style—is generally very accommodating; he will clean, scale and leave the fish whole, or skin and fillet it for you as you wish, so all you have to do is find a good recipe and do the cooking without being bothered by the more tedious task of preliminary preparations.

One final point about choosing fish is that it must be fresh; this is very important, as it goes off very rapidly. The usual rules are that its eyes should be clear and full, not sunken; that its gills should be bright red; that the body should be firm, not flabby; and that it should smell pleasantly fresh, not with a disagreeable odour.

Braised fish steak

This is an excellent way of cooking cod or halibut pieces, or any kind of white fish that is big enough to be cut into cubes 1–1½ in (25–40 mm) square. The most important thing to remember is that the flesh of most fish is very delicate, and if cooked too long over too high a heat will lose its flavour and texture. Treat fish like the tenderest cuts of beef or veal.

    ¾ lb (340 g) fish steak
    1–2 spring onions
    1 slice ginger root
    2 tablespoons soya sauce
    2 tablespoons sherry (or dry white wine)
    1 tablespoon sugar
    2 teaspoons cornflour
    enough oil or lard for shallow-frying

Cut the fish into cubes—not too small, otherwise they break easily when cooked; dry them thoroughly with a cloth or kitchen paper. Finely chop the ginger root and spring onions.

Now heat up the oil or lard in a pan and throw in the ginger and onions, followed almost immediately by the fish cubes. Stir very gently to make sure they do not stick together; now add the sherry or wine, let it bubble for a few seconds and then add the soya sauce, diluted with the same amount of water. Bring it back to the boil, add the sugar and turn down the heat. Let it simmer for 5–10 minutes, depending on the type of fish you use, or until the juice is almost entirely evaporated. Just before serving, mix the cornflour with a little water and pour it over the fish as you bring up the heat again to thicken the gravy.

Fried fish fingers

Are you surprised by the name of this dish? Strictly speaking, it is called 'fish stripes' in Chinese, but I thought 'fish fingers' sounded more homely. In fact there is no reason why you should not use a packet of frozen fish fingers for this recipe; it will save you a lot of preparation and the result will be just the same, for it is the sauce that makes the dish.

¾ lb (340 g) fish fillets (or 14–16 fish fingers)
1–2 spring onions
1 clove garlic
1 slice ginger root
plain flour or breadcrumbs for coating
enough oil for deep-frying

For the sauce:
1 tablespoon soya sauce
1 tablespoon sherry
1 tablespoon vinegar
1 tablespoon sugar
¼ teaspoon monosodium glutamate
a little stock or water

Use cod or halibut or any other white fish that you can cut into long, thin strips like fingers. Finely chop the ginger root and garlic, and cut the spring onions into short pieces about 1-in (25-mm) long. Make the sauce by mixing in a bowl the sherry, sugar, vinegar, soya sauce and monosodium glutamate together with a little stock or water (if using packeted fish fingers, reduce the quantity of soya sauce by half and omit the monosodium glutamate altogether).

While you wait for the oil to heat up, coat the fish strips with flour or breadcrumbs. Deep-fry the fish until they are golden—reduce the heat as soon as you put the fish in hot oil, otherwise they will burn before they are cooked—then drain.

Now heat up a little oil in another pan, first fry the garlic, ginger root, and spring onion for a short while, and then put in the fish fingers, followed by the sauce mixture. Stir until everything is well blended: the fish should be cripsy outside and tender inside, and I promise you it will make ordinary fish fingers taste like something exceptional from an expensive restaurant!

Fried fish slices

After fish cubes and fish fingers, perhaps you would like to try fish slices for a change. To save you the bother of cutting fish into thin slices, you could use fillets of flatfish such as plaice or sole.

½ lb (225 g) fish fillets
1 spring onion
1 clove garlic
1 tablespoon sherry
2–3 tablespoons oil
For coating:
1 egg white
a little cornflour
a little salt

Cut the fish into small, thin slices and coat them with the egg white, followed by a little salt and cornflour.

Heat up the oil in a frying-pan and gently fry the fish slices, using a pair of chopsticks or a fork to separate them; when the colour turns to golden, scoop them out with a perforated spoon and drain.

There should be about 1 tablespoon of oil left in the pan—if too much, pour some out. Throw in the finely chopped garlic and spring onions, followed by the fish slices; add the sherry and the remains of the coating mixture, tilt and turn the pan round slowly at an angle so that the juice covers the fish evenly, and serve. Try not to break up the slices when dishing them out.

Smaller fish under 2 lb (900 g) weight, particularly freshwater fish, are best cooked whole. No formal Chinese dinner is regarded as complete without a whole fish as part of the main course, which usually consists of a whole chicken or duck, a leg or shoulder of pork and the fish, served whole with its head and tail. All these are cooked in rich sauces and with dressings of one kind or another —for this is the cook's chance of showing off his or her skill in presentation; it is the *pièce de résistance*.

If you can get freshwater fish such as carp, perch or rainbow trout, so much the better; if not, sea bass, sea bream, grey mullet or red mullet will do just as well, only their meat is not quite so delicate as that of freshwater fish.

In China, apart from the vegetarians, everyone eats meat, but there are quite a number of people who dislike fish as food. My father is one of them, while my mother positively prefers fish to meat, and the rest of the family seems to be divided half and half—I being strongly on my mother's side. I was told that when my mother was expecting me, she had a longing for freshwater fish, which happened to be rather short in the market in Peking that winter, and I have always believed that was why I like fish so much. One day, when I was about six or seven years old and was travelling with my nanny on one of the small inland rivers in China, the boatman caught a beautiful carp (or was it a perch? I cannot be sure). He cooked it for our lunch, and it was the tastiest fish I have ever eaten. To this day I can still recall vividly the simply cooked fish with its delicious gravy, but everything else about the journey I have completely forgotten, except that I remember my nanny remarked afterwards that nothing could excel river fish cooked with river water. How right she was!

Red-cooked carp

The commonest freshwater fish in China must be the carp, and red-cooking must be about the most usual method of cooking any fish. Carp is a beautiful silver-grey fish. It has become the symbol of good fortune, so it is a must for the traditional New Year celebrations, wedding feasts or any other festivity.

The carp was first imported into Britain in the early seventeenth century and was not introduced into the USA until 1876, but it has since become very abundant there. It is also a favourite fish with Jewish and Central European cooks, and is now widely bred in special farms in Israel.

The ideal size of the carp for this recipe is about 1½ lb (680 g) in weight or a little more. It is cooked whole with its head and tail on. Ask your fishmonger to clean and scale it for you if you are not sure how to do it yourself, and try to cook it the day you buy it, as it does not keep too well—this, of course, applies to almost all fresh fish.

1 carp (1½–2 lb, 680–900 g)
2 spring onions
2 slices ginger root
4–5 tablespoons oil

For the sauce:
3–4 tablespoons soya sauce
3–4 tablespoons sherry
1 teaspoon sugar
2 tablespoons stock or water

Scale the carp (if not already done), wash it under the cold tap and dry it well both inside and out with a cloth or kitchen paper. Trim the fins and tail if not already trimmed, and slash both sides of the fish diagonally as far as the bone at intervals of about ¼ in (6 mm) with a sharp knife. In case you wonder why it is necessary to slash both sides of the fish before cooking, the reason is twofold: first, if you cook the fish whole, the skin will burst unless it is scored; and second, it allows the heat to penetrate more quickly and at the same time helps to diffuse the flavour of seasoning and sauce. Also, as the Chinese never use a knife at the table, it is much easier to serve when you can pick up the pieces of flesh with just a pair of chopsticks.

Cut the spring onions into 1-in (25-mm) lengths. Mix the ingredients of the sauce in a bowl.

Heat up a pan and pour in the oil. Let it get really hot—this will take about 2 minutes—and turn down the heat a little before frying the carp for about 2 minutes on each side, so as not to burn the skin. Now remove the fish and pour off some of the oil, but leave about 1 tablespoon; then bring up the heat again and throw in the spring onions and ginger and the sauce mixture, followed once again by the fish. Now let it simmer for about 10 minutes and serve it on a long dish; but do be careful when removing the carp from the pan; it will not do if you break the fish, for not only will it look bad, it will not taste the same either!

Carp with sweet and sour sauce

Fish cooked with a sweet and sour sauce is very popular in China—far more so than the world-famous pork. The reason must be that most people do not like the smell of fish cooking, and a pungent sauce helps to disguise it somewhat.

There are several varieties of this recipe, but the one below is about the simplest I have come across. A more complicated one is given later (p. 147). If you cannot get a carp, substitute perch, sea bass or grey mullet.

1 carp (1½–2 lb, 680–900 g)
plain flour for coating
enough oil for deep-frying
a little salt

For the sauce:
3 tablespoons sugar
2 tablespoons white wine vinegar
2 tablespoons stock or water
1 tablespoon soya sauce
a little cornflour

Wash and trim the fish as in the previous recipe, dry it thoroughly and slash both sides diagonally at intervals. Rub a little salt both inside and out, then coat the whole fish from head to tail with flour.

Deep-fry the fish in hot oil until golden brown; this will take about 4–5 minutes, and while this is happening, and if you are an experienced cook, mix the sauce in a bowl—but if you are a comparative beginner, then you ought to concentrate all your attention on the fish, in which case mix the sauce beforehand.

When the fish is cooked, drain it well and place it—carefully—on a warmed long dish. Now pour off most of the oil, but leave about 1 tablespoon in the pan and let it get hot again before putting in the sauce mixture; stir this constantly until it bubbles and thickens, then pour it over the fish and serve.

Braised perch à la maison

The perch is considered in China as one of the best freshwater fish. Its flesh is more delicate than that of the carp, and in flavour it resembles river trout. There is a different species in America, called the perch-trout, and another relative is the black bass. (The word 'bass' is derived from 'barse', the old English name for the perch.) In this recipe you can easily use trout instead of perch but probably you will have to use two, as they are much smaller than perch.

    1 perch (1½–2 lb, 680–900 g)
    2 oz (50 g) lean pork or cooked ham
    1–2 spring onions
    1 slice ginger root
    4–5 tablespoons oil

For the sauce:
    1 tablespoon soya sauce
    1 tablespoon yellow bean sauce
    1 tablespoon sherry
    ½ pt (280 ml) stock or water

Wash, trim and slash the fish as in the previous recipes. Slice the pork or ham into thin strips. (You may think this combination of fish and meat rather strange, but the Chinese believe the two flavours blend with each other to their mutual advantage, as you will soon discover for yourself.)

Next cut the spring onions and ginger root into 1-in (25-mm) lengths, and mix the sauce ingredients in a bowl.

Now heat up the oil until it smokes; fry the fish on both sides for about 4 minutes or until the colour of the skin turns golden, then remove and drain.

Leave a little oil in the pan and stir-fry the meat for a while, add the sauce mixture, stir and put the fish back. Bring it to the boil, then put on the lid, reduce the heat and simmer for about 10 minutes; garnish with finely chopped spring onion and serve.

Any left-overs are best eaten cold; warmed-up fish dishes tend to lose much of their delicacy and it brings out the disagreeable fishy smells caused by overcooking. At any rate, the gravy will set into jelly the next day and is very delicious just on its own—it used to be a favourite of mine as a child.

Fresh and seawater shellfish are, as you can well imagine, highly thought of in China. The most common ones are prawns, shrimps and crabs.

The season for crabs is rather short (usually from May to September). Choose a crab which is not too small; otherwise there will be more shell than meat in proportion to its size—but if it is too large, the meat tends to be tough. The female or hen crabs contain a yellowish roe rather like the yolk of an egg, called 'berry' in England—this is highly appreciated in China for its characteristic crab flavour. But unfortunately the crab meat you buy in a tin or frozen packet has had this delicious roe removed. When you buy a fresh crab from the fishmonger and if you are lucky enough to pick out a female or hen crab, make sure you get the 'yolk' or 'berry' after you have asked him to crack open the body and claws for you.

Crab with spring onions and ginger

This is an excellent way of cooking crab in its shell. It is best accompanied by a medium-dry sherry, for ordinary table wine has not the strength to sustain this highly flavoured dish.

2 medium-sized crabs (about ¾ lb, 680 g, each)
2 eggs
4–5 spring onions
4–5 slices ginger root
3–4 tablespoons oil
1 tablespoon sherry
1 teaspoon sugar
a little salt

Break off the legs and crack the claws of the crabs if the fishmonger has not already done so. Wash off any mud or green matter both outside and in the shell, and discard the feathery gills.

Cut the spring onions into 1-in (25-mm) lengths, finely chop the ginger root and beat up the eggs with a little salt.

Now heat up the oil in a large pan, wait for it to smoke and then fry the crabs, stirring constantly until the colour turns bright red. Add the spring onions, ginger, salt, sugar and sherry, and continue stirring for a while; then pour the beaten eggs all over the crabs, stir gently and serve just before the eggs become solid.

Fu yung crab

Most people know that in a Chinese restaurant, *fu yung* means 'omelette', but strictly speaking it means 'white lotus purée' in Chinese, because only the white of the eggs is used to make a lightly scrambled, creamy mixture.

This famous Peking dish originally calls for the white of the eggs with the 'yolk' of the female or hen crab. Since it is rather difficult to get hold of crab 'yolk' nowadays, I have taken the liberty of adapting the recipe somewhat by using the white crab meat and keeping in the yolk of the eggs—there is real compromise for you!

¼ lb (100 g) white crab meat
6 eggs
1 spring onion
1 slice ginger root
1 tablespoon sherry
1 teaspoon sugar
enough oil or lard for shallow-frying
a little stock or water
a little salt

If you are using frozen crab meat, make sure it is defrosted at room temperature for at least 2 hours—never try the short-cut way of soaking it in hot water, which will spoil much of its special flavour. For this recipe you can also use canned crab meat; in this case drain it and discard the soft little bones. Break up the meat into small pieces and mix it with the yolks of the eggs and a little salt.

Finely chop the spring onion and ginger root. Lightly beat up the whites of the eggs with a little salt.

Heat up the oil or lard in a pan, throw in the spring onion and ginger, followed by the crab meat, add sugar, sherry and a little stock or water, stir and let it bubble for a little while; then pour the egg whites over it and blend them well so that it forms a creamy consistency. Do not overcook, being particularly careful about this if you use canned crab meat.

Fried prawns

Fresh prawns and shrimps are grey and almost translucent until cooked, when they turn pink. The larger variety, known as Pacific or king or Dublin Bay prawns, are usually sold in their shells without the heads; the smaller ones are usually sold ready-cooked, and there are also frozen prawns already peeled.

½ lb (225 g) Pacific or king prawns
1 egg white
½ lb (225 g) oil or lard
a little sherry
a little salt
a little cornflour

Wash the prawns, shell and dry them thoroughly with kitchen paper, then use a sharp knife to make a shallow incision down the back of the prawn and pull out the black intestinal vein. Cut each prawn in half. Mix in a little salt, the egg white and a little cornflour and marinate them in the refrigerator for 1–2 hours.

Put a pan over a high heat, and when it is hot, put in the oil or lard. Do not let this get too hot before putting in the prawns. Stir to separate them and scoop them out with a perforated spoon after only a few seconds. Pour out excess oil, leaving a small amount at the bottom of the pan, and put the prawns back together with a little sherry and salt. Stir a few more times and then it is done. The prawns should be bright pink and be so tender as almost to melt in your mouth.

Phoenix tail prawns

These prawns are deep-fried with their tail shells still attached, which is decorative and makes them easy to handle.

½ lb (225 g) Pacific or king prawns
1 spring onion
1 slice ginger root
enough oil for deep-frying
a little sherry
a little lard
a little salt

For coating:
2 egg whites
a little cornflour
a little plain flour
some breadcrumbs

For serving:
lettuce leaves for garnish
1 tablespoon salt
1 tablespoon pepper

Wash and shell the prawns, but leave the tail pieces firmly attached. Split them in half lengthwise and discard the black intestinal vein. Dry the prawns thoroughly with kitchen paper and mix them with a little salt, sherry and lard together with finely chopped spring onion and ginger root.

Now beat up the egg whites really well for at least 30 seconds and fold in a little cornflour.

Heat up quite a lot of oil in a pan or a deep-fryer. Dip each prawn first in plain flour, next in egg white and lastly in breadcrumbs, then drop them into the boiling hot oil and reduce the heat slightly to prevent the prawns from getting burnt. Depending on the size of pan or the amount of oil you use, you can fry several prawns at a time, but make sure they do not stick together. When the colour turns to golden brown, scoop them out with a perforated spoon and drain them on absorbent paper. To serve, arrange them neatly on a bed of lettuce leaves, and eat them with salt and pepper dip, which is made by mixing equal portions of salt and freshly ground pepper and heating them for 2–3 minutes in a dry pan.

'Agitated' prawns

This dish would go well with 'agitated' kidney flowers (see recipe on p. 123, where the name is also explained).

½ lb (225 g) uncooked, unshelled prawns
a few thin slices ginger root
a little sherry
a little sesame seed oil
a little salt

Wash, shell and de-vein the prawns as described in the previous recipes, then cut them into thin slices.

Next boil some water and throw in the prawn slices; in a short while the colour will turn to white. Immediately drain the prawns into a sieve and run cold water over them for a few seconds, then place them on a serving-dish.

Now mix some sherry, salt and sesame seed oil and pour it over the prawns, adding a few thin slivers of ginger root. Leave it to marinate for a while before serving.

Prawn balls assembly

In this dish the prawn balls are first deep-fried in advance, then assembled with the rest of the ingredients just before serving.

½ lb (225 g) uncooked, unshelled prawns
2 oz (50 g) fresh pork fat
½ lb any seasonal green vegetables
2 oz (50 g) bamboo shoots (optional)
1 egg white
1 tablespoon sherry
1¼ tablespoons cornflour

7 fl oz (200 ml) stock
enough oil for deep-frying
a little salt

Wash, shell and de-vein the prawns as in the previous recipes. Chop the prawns and pork fat together until they form a smooth paste, then mix it with the egg white and 1 teaspoon each of cornflour and sherry.

Heat up some oil in a deep-frying-pan—if you have a *wok*, not so much oil is required. When the oil is near boiling point, turn down the heat and use a teaspoon to scoop up a spoonful of the prawn mixture and form a ball about the size of a walnut, then drop it into the hot oil. Fry 4 or 5 balls at a time until they become golden, which should take less than 2–3 minutes. Scoop them out with a perforated spoon or strainer and repeat until all the mixture is used up.

Wash and cut up the vegetables, slice the bamboo shoots, stir-fry them in a little hot oil with salt, then add the prawn balls together with a little more sherry and about a cupful of stock, bring it to the boil, then slowly pour in 1 tablespoon of cornflour ready-mixed with cold water, stirring gently all the time to thicken the gravy—but be careful not to overcook. Serve hot.

Prawns in shells

Another popular cold dish from Shanghai, fresh prawns cooked in their shells are ideal for 'wine-accompanying'. You will find that even a red wine (but not claret) can be served with this dish.

½ lb (225 g) Pacific or king prawns
2 spring onions
2 slices ginger root
2 tablespoons soya sauce
2 tablespoons sherry
1 tablespoon sugar
enough oil for deep-frying
parsley for garnish

Wash and trim off the legs of the prawns, but keep the body shells on. Then fry them in hot oil for a few seconds only, and as soon as they start to turn pink, scoop them out with a perforated spoon.

Now pour off the oil, then return the prawns to the pan and add the soya sauce, sherry and sugar with the finely chopped spring onions and ginger root. Stir vigorously for a little while, then it is done. Before serving, garnish it with finely chopped fresh parsley.

When eating, you put the whole prawn in your mouth, suck the sauce and at the same time extract the meat off its shell. This is easily done if you use chopsticks rather than a spoon or fork. If your guests are unfamiliar with chopsticks, then urge them to use their fingers instead.

Sesame seed prawn toast

Those of you who have been to a Chinese restaurant serving Peking-style food will probably have been delighted by this delicious dish. It is in fact quite simple and easy to make, and would no doubt equally delight and impress your guests.

$\frac{1}{4}$ lb (100 g) uncooked prawns
$\frac{1}{4}$ lb (100 g) fish fillets (cod, plaice, etc)
2 eggs
4 large slices white bread
enough oil for deep-frying
3 tablespoons breadcrumbs
3 tablespoons sesame seeds
a little salt
a little pepper

Wash, shell and de-vein the prawns, then finely chop them with the fish to form a creamy paste; add a little salt and pepper and mix well together with the white of 1 egg in a bowl.

Slice the bread as thinly as you can, remove the crusts and toast it lightly. Cut each slice into 6 or 8 fingers. Beat up the egg yolk with the other egg in a bowl, and mix the breadcrumbs and sesame seeds on a plate.

Now spread each toasted finger with a generous layer of prawn mixture, then dip it in the beaten egg before coating it with breadcrumbs and sesame seeds. When you have done 5 or 6 fingers in this manner, put them in a wire basket and deep-fry them in hot oil for about 2 minutes or until they start to turn golden. Drain and keep them on a hot plate. After you have fried all the fingers, then put them all together in the wire basket and deep-fry them for a further minute or so to crisp them. Drain and serve them, they should taste wonderful—'Out of this world', my young daughter would say!

If you have difficulty in obtaining sesame seeds, they can be omitted, in which case double the amount of breadcrumbs used. They will still taste delicious, though not with quite the same aroma.

Fish slices and mushrooms assembly

This dish is not unlike the French *Filets de Sole Bonne Femme* (sole with mushrooms and wine sauce), but I think you will agree that the Chinese method is much simpler.

>   1 lb (450 g) fillet of fish (cod, plaice, sole or turbot)
>   ½ lb (225 g) white mushrooms
>   1 egg white
>   ½ pt (280 ml) dry white wine
>   enough oil for shallow-frying
>   1½ teaspoons salt
>   1½ teaspoons sugar
>   a little pepper
>   a little plain flour
>   a little cornflour

Cut the fish into slices roughly the same size, mix in ½ teaspoon each of salt and sugar, a little freshly ground pepper and the egg white; then coat each piece lightly in flour and shallow-fry them on both sides gently over a moderate heat until golden. Drain and place them on a plate.

Slice the mushrooms and fry them with 1 teaspoon each of salt and sugar, a little pepper and the dry white wine. Simmer for a few minutes, then thicken the sauce with a little cornflour mixed in cold water, pour it over the fish and serve.

'Smoked' fish

The interesting thing about this dish is that the fish is not smoked.
It acquires a smoky taste from being first deep-fried in hot oil, then
marinated in the specially prepared sauce.

    1 lb (450 g) cod steaks (or any other firm white fish)
    2 spring onions
    2 slices ginger root
    2 tablespoons soya sauce
    2 tablespoons sherry
    1 tablespoon brown sugar
    ½ teaspoon salt
    ¼ teaspoon Five Spice powder
    ½ pt (280 ml) stock or water
    enough oil for deep-frying (at least 1 pt, 570 ml)

First cut the fish into small pieces about the size of a matchbox, mix
in the soya sauce, sherry and salt, and marinate for not less than 30
minutes.

Before cooking the fish, remove the pieces from the marinade.
Add to the marinade the finely chopped spring onions, ginger root,
stock or water, brown sugar and Five Spice powder; bring this
mixture to the boil, then reduce the heat to its lowest point and let it
simmer gently for 10 minutes or so, then strain through a sieve and
keep the sauce.

Heat up the oil in a deep frying-pan or *wok* until very hot (you
will see a haze forming above the surface of the oil), drop in the fish
pieces a few at a time and fry for about 5 minutes or until they are
crisp and golden, then pick them out with chopsticks or a perforated
spoon and dip them in the sauce for a while before laying them out
side by side on a dish to cool.

Sweet and sour fish

Fish cooked whole always looks impressive, and is a must for any feast, big or small. If you have already successfully tried out the recipe for carp with sweet and sour sauce (p. 137), then you will have no difficulty at all in preparing this dish, for as you will see, the basic method is the same.

    1 perch or grey mullet (1½–2 lb, 680–900 g)
    1 green pepper
    2 carrots
    1–2 sticks celery
      (Or:
    1 bamboo shoot
    3–4 water chestnuts
    2–3 Wooden Ears)
    2–3 spring onions
    2 slices ginger root
    1 clove garlic
    2–3 tablespoons white wine vinegar
    5–6 tablespoons oil
    a little plain flour
    a little salt

For the sauce:
    3 tablespoons sugar
    2 tablespoons soya sauce
    2 tablespoons sherry
    2 teaspoons cornflour
    ¼ pt (140 ml) stock or water
    a little chilli sauce (optional)

Clean, scale and score the fish as described in the earlier whole fish recipes. Dry it thoroughly with a cloth or kitchen paper before rubbing it with salt both inside and out, then coat the whole fish from head to tail with flour.

Slice very thinly the green pepper, carrots and celery (or bamboo shoots and water chestnuts, and the Wooden Ears previously soaked in warm water for about 20 minutes). Shred the spring onions and ginger root in the size of matchsticks, and finely chop the garlic. Mix all the ingredients of the sauce.

Heat the oil in a frying-pan or *wok* until it smokes and fry the fish for about 3 or 4 minutes on both sides, or until golden and crisp. Be careful when turning the fish over, and use a wide-bladed tool, so that it is kept in one piece and the skin is not broken. Drain and place it on a heated long dish.

Pour off some of the oil from the pan, so that there is only about 2 tablespoons left, and fry the spring onions, ginger root and garlic, followed almost immediately by the vegetables. Add a little salt and the wine vinegar. Stir all the time, then add in the stock mixture to form a thickish sauce. Pour the vegetables with the sauce over the fish and serve immediately.

Fish head soup

It is fitting and traditional to end a banquet with a dish that is simplicity itself. Nothing is simpler or easier to make than this soup, which is made out of the remains of the main course of the feast.

Head, tail and left-overs from a whole fish

1 pt (570 ml) stock
1 spring onion
a little parsley
a little vinegar
a little pepper

Traditionally, use the head and tail with any other left-overs from sweet and sour fish. First break up the bone and crush the head into smaller pieces, then add some stock made out of bones (chicken, pork, etc), bring it to the boil and simmer for 10 minutes or so.

To serve, place in a large bowl a little finely chopped spring onion and fresh parsley, add some vinegar and pepper, then pour the boiling soup into it. Serve hot. It is most delicious!

Of course you should have no difficulty in choosing a suitable wine for any of these fish dishes. As everybody knows, white wine goes best with fish, but do not rule out the possibility of red altogether. For instance, a cool, fresh Beaujolais will go very nicely with most of these dishes, and the more strongly flavoured dishes such as the fried fish slices, braised perch à la maison, and crab with spring onion and ginger all require something a little fuller than ordinary table wine. I suggest that you try a medium-dry sherry. An amontillado is very similar both in taste and body to the Chinese 'yellow wine' made of glutinous rice, which is the most popular drink in many parts of China.

VIII
First Catch Your Duck

Roast duck Peking style
Gold and silver duck
Duck liver in wine sauce
Braised duck liver

Duck giblets assembly
Braised duck
Roast duck Canton style
Duck soup

If I were asked to name one single dish as the best example of *haute cuisine* in China, the choice would be difficult, but after a little hesitation, I would eventually decide on Peking duck.

This unique dish owns its worldwide reputation not so much for the way it is cooked, which could be very simply, but also for the way it is eaten. Another important factor lies in the specially reared species of duck used. To start with, it has a different appearance from the common duck and is brought by several stages of force-feeding and care to exactly the right degree of plumpness and tenderness before it is prepared for the oven.

As you will realise, Peking duck is, strictly speaking, not a home dish, but since most Western kitchens are equipped with an oven, there is no reason why you should not try to cook it at home. The original Chinese recipe runs on for pages, starting with a detailed description of how to make up the duck feed, and continuing with complicated instructions on how to build and fire the oven; there is also an important aspect of the preparation: the killing of the duck. It starts off, literally, with 'First catch your duck!' Then it goes on to say: 'With your left hand get hold of both wings of the duck, using your little finger to hook up the right foot of the duck, meanwhile using your thumb and index finger to press down on the duck's neck; and with the knife in your right hand . . .' I think I will spare you the rest of the gory details.

Since it is almost impossible to obtain genuine Peking duck outside China, I have modified the Chinese recipe somewhat, and I can assure you that the result is entirely satisfactory.

Roast duck Peking style

1 duckling (3½–4 lb, 1·6–1·8 kg)

For cooking (optional):
1 tablespoon sugar
1 teaspoon salt
½ pt (280 ml) water

For the sauce:
3 tablespoons yellow bean sauce
2 tablespoons sugar   } or substitute 6 table-
1 tablespoon sesame seed oil (or olive oil) } spoons Hoi Sin sauce

For serving:
24 thin pancakes (see p. 95)
10 spring onions
½ cucumber

Try to get a fresh (not frozen) oven-ready duckling not less than
3½ lb (1·6 kg) in weight—the smaller the duck, the less the meat; but
if the duck is over 5 lb (2·3 kg), the meat will be too tough. There is
very little to do except to clean it and hang it up to dry thoroughly,
preferably overnight in a draught (or use a fan heater or even a
hairdryer). This is most important, as the drier the skin, the crispier
the duck when roasted, and this is one of the main characteristics
of this dish.

In order to make the skin appear golden as well as crispy it is
advisable to coat the duck with a mixture of sugar, salt and water
before drying. To do this you mix 1 tablespoon of sugar with 1 teaspoon of salt in ½ pt (280 ml) of water and rub the duck with this
mixture several hours before cooking.

When the duck is thoroughly dry, place it on the middle rack of a
preheated oven (400° F, 200° C, gas mark 6) and roast for just over
1 hour—add an extra 10 minutes for every extra 1 lb (450 g) over
4 lb (1·8 kg).

While the duck is being roasted (there is nothing to be done to
it, no basting nor turning over), you can make the thin pancakes,
using the recipe on p. 95, and the sauce. This is simply done by
mixing the yellow bean sauce, sugar and sesame seed oil (or olive oil)
over a gentle heat for 2 or 3 minutes. Next cut the spring onions

into 2–3-in (50–75-mm) lengths and slice the cucumber into thin strips of the same size. All these accompaniments are served in separate dishes, and the duck is carved at the table, with the skin and meat in separate dishes.

To eat, you help yourself to a pancake, and on it you spread a teaspoon or so of sauce, then place a few cucumber and spring onion pieces in the middle, and on top of these you add a piece or two of the sliced duck meat with a piece or two of the crispy skin. Now roll up the pancake like a sausage roll, turning up the bottom end to prevent anything dropping out.

The combination of the crunchy vegetables, the crispy skin and tender meat with the sweet sauce, all at the same time, is indescribable.

The carcass of the duck is crushed to make a soup with cabbage to be served at the end of the meal (p. 161). There is very little waste in cooking a duck: almost everything is used as ingredients of a number of delicious dishes. (The most famous duck restaurant in Peking, Pien Yi Fang, offers more than a hundred different dishes on the menu, entirely based on parts of duck. But most of these are far beyond our scope; for instance, one recipe calls for thirty duck tongues!)

Gold and silver duck

This is an ideal way of using up any left-overs from the roast duck— though you are most unlikely to have any, unless your guests failed to turn up! The main ingredients of this dish are duck and ham: the pale colour of the duck offsets the pinkness of the ham, forming a pretty pattern when arranged on a serving-plate—hence the name of this dish.

½ lb (225 g) duck meat
½ lb (225 g) cooked ham
2 teaspoons gelatine
4 tablespoons sherry
½ pt (280 ml) stock or water
a little salt
a little pepper

Try to slice both duck and ham into pieces roughly the same size —say not larger than a matchbox—and arrange them alternately in several layers on a deep, long dish. Sprinkle them with a little salt and pepper. Dissolve the gelatine in hot stock or water with the sherry. When the gelatine is completely dissolved (this is most important, as otherwise it will not set; detailed instructions are normally given on each packet of gelatine), pour it all over the duck and ham, and refrigerate it to set. Turn it out on to another long dish for serving, either as an *hors d'oeuvre*, or as a part of a buffet.

Duck liver in wine sauce

This is another cold dish, and therefore ideal to be served as a starter, or what the Chinese call a 'wine-accompanying' dish.

- 1 lb (450 g) duck liver
- 2 tablespoons sherry
- 2 tablespoons brandy
- 1 tablespoon sugar
- 1 teaspoon salt
- a little monosodium glutamate (optional)
- 7 fl oz (200 ml) stock or water

Wash and clean the liver well, trimming off any part that has been discoloured by the gall bladder. Cover the liver with cold water in a pan and bring it to the boil, then drain and discard the water.

Next mix together the sherry, brandy, sugar, salt, monosodium glutamate (optional), and stock or water; add the parboiled liver and bring it to the boil; simmer gently for about 10 minutes, then take the liver out to cool.

To serve, cut the liver into thin slices and arrange them in neat rows on a plate; pour over it the remains of the sauce, which should have been reduced to no more than a couple of tablespoons.

Braised duck liver

Another 'wine-accompanying' dish, but this time it is served hot. Instead of duck liver you can use almost any other liver—chicken, pig, lamb or calf—the method of cooking is basically the same.

1 lb (450 g) duck liver
2 oz (50 g) bamboo shoots
½ oz (15 g) Chinese dried mushrooms (or ¼ lb, 100 g, fresh mushrooms)
1–2 spring onions
1–2 slices ginger root
2 tablespoons soya sauce
2 tablespoons sherry
1 tablespoon brown sugar
1 tablespoon yellow bean sauce
enough oil for shallow-frying
a little pepper
a little stock or water

Wash and clean the liver well, blanch in boiling water and drain, then cut it into ¼-in (6-mm) wide strips.

Slice the bamboo shoots and mushrooms (if using dried ones, soak them in warm water for about 30 minutes first) and finely chop the spring onions and ginger root (you only need a small amount of each).

To cook, first heat up a little oil in a pan, and before it gets too hot, put in the brown sugar; stir until it starts to bubble, then add the soya sauce, sherry, spring onions, ginger root and pepper, followed immediately by the bamboo shoots and mushrooms. Blend well and cook for a short while, then take it off the heat.

Next heat up a little more oil, and before it gets too hot, put in the yellow bean sauce and stir for a few seconds before putting in the liver and returning the bamboo shoots and mushrooms. Add a little stock, continue stirring and cook over a high heat until the juice is reduced by half. Scoop out the liver and place it on a warmed serving-dish, let the juice bubble away until it is reduced by half again, then pour it over the liver and serve.

It should taste tender and delicious!

Duck giblets assembly

The ingredients for this recipe are not unlike those of stir-fried ten varieties (i) (p. 78), but the method is somewhat different.

giblets (gizzards and hearts only) from 2–3 ducks (or chickens)
2 oz (50 g) bamboo shoots
½ oz (15 g) Chinese dried mushrooms (or ¼ lb, 100 g, fresh mushrooms)
1 cos lettuce (or ½ lb, 225 g, green cabbage)
1 tablespoon soya sauce
1 tablespoon sherry
enough oil for shallow-frying
a little stock
a little cornflour
a little salt

Slit the gizzards on the curved side, open them and remove the
inner bags, taking care not to break them as they are full of grit.
Sometimes this has already been done, so all you have to do is clean
and wash them well. Trim off the excess fat from the upper parts of
the hearts.

First place the giblets in cold water and bring it to the boil, then
plunge them in cold water before cutting them into thin slices.

Slice the bamboo shoots, mushrooms, lettuce or cabbage. If using
fresh mushrooms, blanch them; also blanch the lettuce or cabbage,
drain and put them aside.

Next heat up some oil in a pan, put in the giblets with bamboo
shoots, mushrooms and greens, a little salt and the soya sauce, sherry
and stock, bring it to the boil then reduce the heat and simmer for
a few minutes. Just before serving, thicken the gravy with a little
cornflour—not too thick, otherwise it will spoil the appearance of
the translucent glaze.

Braised duck

In China, duck is second only to chicken in popularity as a poultry
dish. While chicken is more of an everyday food, duck is something
special, a must for festivities and feasts. As I mentioned earlier, not
many Chinese homes are equipped with a Western-type oven, and
therefore stewing or braising is by far the most widely used cooking
method for poultry in China.

1 duckling (4½–5 lb, 2·0–2·3 kg)
1 small leek (or 2–3 spring onions)
4 tablespoons soya sauce
4 tablespoons sherry
2 slices ginger root
2 oz (50 g) rock candy or crystallized sugar
½ orange

Clean the duck thoroughly and place the finely chopped leek or spring onions and ginger root together with the peel of half an orange inside it.

Use a large saucepan or a casserole to boil about 2 pt (1·1 l) of water, put in the duck and boil rapidly for 4–5 minutes, turning it over a few times; then discard two-thirds of the water and add the sherry, soya sauce and candy or sugar. Bring it to the boil again, then put on the lid tightly and simmer gently for 30 minutes, turning the duck over at least once. At this stage you can either continue cooking over a low heat for 1 hour longer or transfer the casserole to a preheated oven (375° F, 190° C, gas mark 5) for 1 hour.

Either serve the duck whole in its own juice, or take it out, cut it into small pieces and garnish it with orange slices.

Roast duck Canton style

Those of you who have been to a good Cantonese restaurant must have tasted those delicious roast ducks seen hanging in the windows. They have a shining reddish-brown skin and are often called 'lacquered ducks'. Strictly speaking, they are not really part of home cooking in China; but since almost every kitchen in the West is equipped with an oven, there is no reason why you should not enjoy this luxury by serving it at your banquet.

1 duckling (4½–5 lb, 2·0–2·3 kg)
a little salt

For the stuffing:
2 spring onions
1 slice ginger root

2 tablespoons sugar
2 tablespoons sherry
1 tablespoon yellow bean sauce
1 tablespoon Hoi Sin sauce
1 tablespoon oil
a little Five Spice powder

For coating:
4 tablespoons honey
1 tablespoon vinegar
½ pt (280 ml) water
a little 'red powder' (or cochineal)

Wash and clean the duck well, then pat it dry inside and out with a cloth or kitchen paper. Rub it inside and out with salt, then tie the neck tightly with string, so that no liquid could drip out when hanging it head down.

To make the stuffing, heat up the oil in a saucepan, mix in the sugar, sherry, bean sauce and Hoi Sin sauce, a little Five Spice powder and the finely chopped spring onions and ginger root. Bring to the boil and blend the mixture well, then pour it into the cavity of the duck and sew it up securely.

Now make the coating by boiling the water and adding the honey, vinegar and a little 'red powder' (or a few drops of cochineal). Mix well.

Next plunge the whole duck into a large pot of boiling water for a few seconds only, take it out and baste it thoroughly with the 'coating' mixture; then hang it up to dry for at least 2–3 hours (use a hairdryer or fan heater to hasten it).

To cook, preheat the oven to 400° F (200° C or gas mark 6), hang the duck head down on a meat hook, and put a tray of cold water at the bottom of the oven to catch the drippings. After 25 minutes or so, reduce the heat to 350° F (180° C, gas mark 4) and roast for a further 30 minutes, basting with the remains of the mixture once or twice during the cooking. When it is done, let it cool a little, then remove the string and pour the liquid stuffing out; it can be used as gravy.

Traditionally, this duck is cut up into small pieces and served cold. But there is no reason why you should not serve it whole and carve it at the table, as it looks most impressive with its 'lacquered' skin all glittering.

Duck soup

This simple dish is traditionally served at the end of a banquet. You will need the carcass of the duck, plus its giblets if you have not already used them for another dish.

1 duck carcass (plus giblets if available)
1 lb (450 g) Chinese cabbage (or any other type of cabbage)
1–2 slices ginger root
a little salt
a little pepper

Break up the carcass, place it together with the giblets and any other bits and pieces in a large pot or pan, cover it with water, add the ginger root, bring it to the boil, skim off the impurities floating on the surface, and let it simmer gently with a lid on for at least 30 minutes. Now add the washed and sliced cabbage, season with salt and pepper, continue cooking for 20 minutes or so, and then it is ready for serving.

Now, is there an easier way of making a more nourishing and delicious soup?

IX
Little Feasts and Grand Banquets

A 'little feast' in China is really only a dinner party. It need not be a special occasion; any excuse, such as the coming of spring, an appointment to a new job or just a reunion of some old friends will do fine. Or in any case, maybe you would like to show off your newly acquired skill. Should you feel slightly nervous about embarking on cooking so many new dishes all at once, why not try out a few beforehand? Trying one or two at a time a few weeks in advance will not only give you the experience you need, but also extra confidence—that is, if the dishes are successful!

With the exception of a formal occasion such as birthday or wedding celebrations, most Chinese dinner parties are of an impromptu nature; usually the invitations are issued at short notice—sometimes only on the morning of the actual day! A special messenger will go round with the guest list and call on various addresses, and each person invited will then tick against his or her name with the word 'known'; this is normally taken to mean that the invitation has been accepted, for otherwise he would indicate a reason for being unable to attend. One advantage of this type of invitation is that you can see at a glance who else will be there, and should you find any *persona non grata* on the list, you can always find some excuse for not being able to accept the invitation.

It is not the general practice to state a precise time for the dinner on the invitation, but guests will start to arrive soon after 6 pm or so, and dinner is normally served at 7 pm, by which time all those invited should have arrived—it would have been bad manners for any guest to turn up at a dinner party after 7 pm in China! Seating arrangements also differ somewhat from the Western convention: the 'head of the table' is the seat facing the entrance and is always reserved for the guest of honour, while the host and hostess are always seated on the opposite side of the table with their backs to the door. The origin of this convention derives from an episode in

F*

the ancient history of China when a certain tyrant was stabbed in the back while being feasted by his enemies. So now the guest of honour, seated facing the door, would be the first person to see the assassin entering the room should the host have any evil intentions!

I am not suggesting that you should follow the Chinese convention of serving your dinner earlier, nor by abandoning your own traditional seating arrangements, but one Chinese custom I would like to urge you to adopt is the attitude regarding food. There are those of us who eat in order to live, and there are those who live in order to eat. In the case of a dinner party, the main objective should be sheer enjoyment, therefore it should be in an informal and relaxed atmosphere. 'Don't stand on ceremony' and 'Please feel at home' should be the true motto of any successful party. If you must 'dress for dinner', then put on something comfortable rather than stiff and tight, so that you can really relax. How can anybody enjoy eating if he is too inhibited by a set of table manners and social etiquette that bears no relationship whatever to the qualities of the food served? Now let us get down to the more serious side of the business, namely the planning of the menu.

A feast for ten or twelve people will consist of at least ten dishes plus soup, rice and a dessert. Normally it starts off with four cold dishes as *hors d'oeuvres*, served simultaneously, followed by four hot dishes served one after another, then soup to clear your palate for the two big dishes served together with rice and finally the dessert.

I do hope you will forgive me for stressing once more the importance of harmony achieved by a well-balanced menu. The points to bear in mind are contrast in taste, texture and colour. So our sample menu will be something like this.

Sliced chicken with ham and broccoli (p. 59)
'Agitated' prawns (p. 143)
'Agitated' kidney flowers (p. 123)
Sweet and sour cucumber (p. 74)

Lotus white chicken (p. 60)
Stir-fried pork and mange-touts (p. 92)
Prawn balls assembly (p. 143)
Eggs with tomatoes (p. 76)

West Lake beef soup (p. 93)

Braised duck (p. 158)
Sweet and sour fish (p. 147)
Boiled rice (p. 28)

Fruit (see p. 42)

The first four dishes are served cold, and therefore can be prepared beforehand, but the rest of the feast, with the exception of the braised duck and rice, all requires last-minute cooking. So a precise schedule is essential, or otherwise your dinner party may turn into a fiasco!

Unless you and your guests are teetotallers, you cannot possibly do without wine for this feast; in fact it will not be a feast at all even though you have spent a lot of trouble in the kitchen.

Most people might be slightly baffled when faced with the task of choosing suitable wine or wines to go with Chinese food, because the usual rule-of-thumb guide does not seem to apply in most cases. For in China, it is not the natural taste of the food, but rather the method in which food is prepared that determines the order of its appearance at the table.

Bearing this point in mind, one can easily deduce from it that the food served will start with light dishes, then gradually progress to heavier and stronger-tasting dishes, sometimes with 'neutral' dishes in between courses to act as a stopgap. Following this factor as a guide, you can now choose your wine for each course without much difficulty. Let us take this feast as an example. To start with, as an apéritif to go with the cold *hors d'oeuvres*, serve any light white wine such as Muscadet, Chablis or Graves, or for those who prefer a less dry white wine, hock or Moselle—in fact, the choice is almost limitless: there is always a wide range of sound and delicate white wines at your disposal. In fact it need not be confined to whites only; for those who like it a rosé, and indeed a sparkling wine or champagne will also be fine.

For the next course, when you are eating the hot fried dishes, a stronger wine with more fruitiness and flavour such as Alsace, Côtes du Rhône, or Pouilly Blanc Fumé should be served, or for those who prefer red wine, Beaujolais, Chinon, Bourgueil or any other light and 'tasty' reds—again the choice is wide.

For the braised duck and sweet and sour fish, of course a more robust wine is called for. What you need is a full-bodied and strongly flavoured red to offset the rather aromatic quality of the food. So for the claret lovers, I would suggest the aromatic, generous yet soft Pomerol, St Émilion or red Graves; but personally I would prefer a firmer and fruitier great burgundy such as Nuits-Saint-Georges, Beaune, or Vosne Romanée. Equally, a powerful and fragrant Châteauneuf-du-Pape or Hermitage will be a success.

When does a feast become a banquet? According to my dictionary, a feast is a sumptuous meal, while a banquet is a sumptuous feast. So there you are!

After the success, or should I say the triumph, of your little feast, what better way to celebrate it than to have a banquet as a follow-up?

The main point to remember in planning your banquet is that you cannot expect good food when cooking in large quantities, so if you are having twenty-four guests instead of twelve, do not double the amount of ingredients used, but rather increase the number of courses so that not only will you achieve a better result, but also there will be a larger variety of different dishes for your guests to marvel at and enjoy. Nor is it necessary to stick to the 'one dish per person' rule. For instance, sixteen dishes should be more than enough for twenty or more people; personally, I think no feast or banquet should exceed sixteen dishes however sumptuous you want it to be; otherwise it would be too much of a waste, both in time and money.

So a sample menu will run very much on the same lines as the little feast: you start off with four cold dishes, such as 'smoked' fish, soya pork, braised eggs and pickled vegetables; then follow up with either four more cold dishes or four 'small' hot dishes to be served simultaneously or two at a time; these dishes are usually stir-fried or deep-fried, but always crisp and dry such as prawn balls, sesame seed prawn toast, soya chicken or duck, etc. This is followed by four more hot dishes, such as diced chicken with green peppers, stir-fried kidney flowers, beef in oyster sauce, chicken wings assembly, meat slices with spring onions, fish slices and mushrooms assembly, etc—but the range here is almost limitless, one can go on almost indefinitely. Now before the final four 'big' dishes, soup is usually served at this point to act as a breather. It should be a light, clear soup, and only a very small portion is required by each guest. The four 'big' dishes would be whole chicken, duck, fish and pork leg or shoulder. This is the main course of the banquet, when the conversation would become subdued and serious eating would commence, for until now all the other dishes have only been a warming-up to get you into the right mood for the final assault. Towards the end of these 'big' dishes, a large bowl of steaming hot soup is served. The soup is usually made out of the bones from the main course with vegetables added. For instance, if Peking duck has been one of the main courses, then the carcass of the duck will be simmered with cabbage to make duck soup; or in the case of sweet and sour fish, the fish head and tail would serve the same purpose. In fact both these soup dishes are classics of their own, a must for any banquet.

My dear readers, I do hope you have enjoyed reading and trying out some of the recipes in this book. I am sure you will agree that there is really no mystery involved in Chinese cooking, once you have learnt the basic principles: that the most important points to remember when selecting ingredients are colour, texture and flavour; that the success of a particular dish depends on the blending and harmonizing of these points; and that, to a large extent, the same applies to planning a menu, where the accent is on harmony and contrast in order to achieve a good balance.

I cannot emphasize enough the importance of fully preparing all the ingredients before the actual cooking, for if you have all the materials well prepared and set out within easy reach, you should feel relaxed and avoid last-minute panic. There is not much point in cooking if you do not enjoy it, so you must reserve peace of mind in order to cook a good meal.

Harold Wilshaw, the cookery writer for *The Guardian*, once said: 'Quite my favourite way of spending any money which comes my way is to have friends round my table, eating my food and drinking my wine. I have no car or television set, and so the money I do not spend on those two boring adjuncts to modern living, I spend giving little luncheons and dinners.' I think he has definitely got the right approach to life, and only wish more people would adopt the same attitude, thus creating a happier world for all of us.

X

The Franco-Chinese Entente—
Wine with Chinese Food

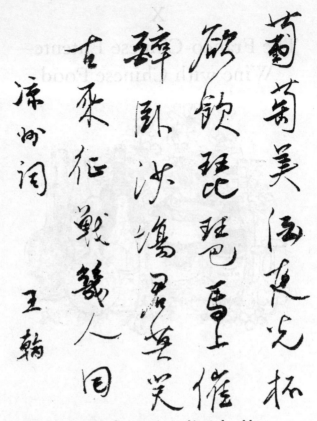

Beautiful grape wine glittering in a white jade goblet:
I was just about to drink it when the lute was sounded, hastening
  me to mount my horse.
Should I lie drunk on the battlefield beyond the Great Wall,
  please don't laugh at me,
For how many warriors have returned home from an expedition
  since the ancient days?

Wang Han: *Song of the Western Region*

I was about seven when my grandfather taught me this eighth-century poem, and it must have been at roughly the same time when I was first introduced to a taste of port wine by my grandmother, whose home-made rice wine had already initiated me into an early fondness for alcohol.

Whether it was the delicious taste of port that influenced my appreciation for this moving passage of the poem, or the spirit of the poem that moved me to enjoy the port at such a tender age, I honestly could not tell. However, I can still recall to this day the sensation that I experienced when I first sipped that ruby-coloured liquid; nor can I ever forget the thrill that greeted me when I encountered that poem. It carried me bodily back over a thousand years beyond the Great Wall, in a state of refined intoxication, lying on a moonlit battlefield, miles away from home—for at that time, because of the war with Japan, we had fled our home town and taken refuge in a Buddhist temple in the hills, some three hundred miles away in Southern China.

Of course, this poem also shows that grape wine has been produced in China for more than a thousand years. In fact it was during the Han dynasty (208 BC–AD 220) that the vine, *Vitis vinifera*, was first introduced into China from Iran, although the art of wine making was not acquired until the early T'ang dynasty in the seventh century, from Turkestan. There is a detailed chapter on the history of the vine in the Far East in the scholarly book *Dionysus*, by Edward Hyams; only he has drawn the wrong conclusion in an otherwise admirably well-written book: that viticulture never really 'took' in China.

Today, if you walk down Gerrard Street in London you will see scores of colourful wine bottles displayed in Chinese shop windows. There is a wide range of varieties, but basically there are only four types: red and white, both sweet and dry. Hugh Johnson is, as far

as I can gather, one of the very few wine writers who appears to appreciate the Chinese products for more than their mere curiosity value. His comment on the dry white from Shantung is: 'Extremely palatable, very dry, with a reasonable scent and a distant cousin-ship of flavour to a light sherry.' I only wish the same could be said about the reds. But alas, the best red, which is sweet, resembles a light tawny port, hardly a 'table' wine in the normal sense.

In an earlier chapter, I mentioned the importance of personal taste in selecting wines to accompany different foods. In Britain, we are fortunate in that, not being a large wine-producing country, there is such a wide range of different wines from all over the world on the market to choose from. You have probably heard how people in certain wine-producing regions will only drink their local wine, be it red or white, sweet or dry, to go with whatever food they eat. There is nothing really wrong in this practice, but since we have the opportunity, why not take advantage of our large choice?

Enough nonsense has been written on wine, which to many people, myself included, is a fascinating subject. What I am propos-ing to do here is not to tell you what wine you should drink with what food, nor do I intend to write an informative chapter on the merits of different wines; all I am doing here is to jot down some personal reminiscences of meals and bottles I have enjoyed over the years, and try to convey some of my pleasure to the reader, if such a thing is possible. You are not expected to agree with everything I have to say, indeed it would be very dull if you do, for I cannot emphasize enough my point of individual taste. Remember the maxim: 'One man's meat is another man's poison', but also bear in mind that unless you are eating and drinking alone, other people's taste must be taken into consideration, for our aim in entertaining is to create general harmony above all else. What little guidance you will find in this chapter is entirely based on my own personal experiences, it is up to you to adapt it to different occasions. Here I would like to quote the late André Simon: 'The connoisseur must be critical and not take for granted that the expert is always right; but he must not be self-opinionated and refuse advice.'

I have been drinking wine since early childhood, but always moderately. The only occasion when I over-indulged myself was when I was four or five years old, and my grandmother let me taste some of her home-made rice wine, which I liked so much that when her back was turned I helped myself from the big urn. To this day I can still recall the aroma that greeted me when I lifted the lid of the wine urn, after climbing up on a footstool, for the urn was as tall as me, and as I peeped down the narrow opening I could see my little face reflected on the surface of the beautiful liquor. What happened after that has become rather blurred. I believe they found me sound asleep at the foot of the wine urn, and it was obvious what had happened. But I do remember there was no scene or punishment—I think the adults were more amused than annoyed, for no real harm had been done. In fact, if anything, I was taught a good lesson by that experience: I have since learnt to restrain myself whenever I come across anything I really like, and thus appreciate it even better.

Sherry

I mentioned earlier that Chinese rice wine is very similar to a medium sherry, both in flavour and body, as well as in colour—for rice wine is commonly called 'yellow wine' in China. Now I am sure you will agree that sherry is a very nice drink, it is liked by almost everyone, for there is quite a range of sherries to meet all tastes, from bone-dry to very sweet. But many people regard sherry as an apéritif only, which is a pity, for a good sherry will taste even better with food; and there are enough varieties to accompany several different courses throughout a meal.

Although sherry is basically a white wine, it goes well not only with fish and chicken dishes, but also all sorts of meat and vegetables, particularly dishes which require a strong and solid drink to offset their rich taste and flavour.

As for 'sherries' made in countries other than Spain, whatever their merits, they remain imitations, though in certain cases not unsuccessful. Sometimes I use a medium-dry Cyprus sherry for cooking, purely for reasons of economics, and the result is quite satisfactory.

Burgundy

If sherry is the ideal white wine for all Chinese food, then I would suggest that a good Beaujolais is the perfect red. I use the word 'good' here to emphasize the importance of careful choice when selecting a Beaujolais. It is said that such is the demand for this wine, that more 'Beaujolais' is drunk in Paris in a year than is produced in the whole district. I find that because of the enormous quantity of Beaujolais produced each year, the quality varies a great deal. Therefore even a genuine Beaujolais can be rather indifferent in some cases. I think it is worth while paying a little extra to buy bottles that bear a *commune* name (and a single vineyard can be even better). My favourites are Juliénas, Fleurie, Morgon, and Côtes de Brouilly, in that order.

What is it that makes Beaujolais so attractive to most people? I think the answer must be because of its light yet firm body, its fragrant and fruity nose, and above all its distinctive flavour which though difficult to describe, is immediately recognizable. Once you have tasted the genuine article, an ordinary 'Beaujolais' will taste either too heavy or too watery, but in either case without much fruit or a very distinctive flavour.

A good red Mâcon probably represents the best value for money, as it is generally cheaper than a Beaujolais but not necessarily inferior (both are made from the Gamay grape). The famous Pouilly Fuissé, a refreshing dry white wine, comes from this district. I find it has a more delicious nose and more depth of flavour than the better-known Chablis farther to the north.

Undoubtedly, the greatest of all white burgundies is Le Montrachet, which comes from the two *communes* of Puligny and Chassagne. I suggest that you should choose the food to eat with it very carefully. Normally it is a question of choosing wine to accompany food, but with Le Montrachet it is the other way round. Avoid dishes that are too spicy or with too rich a sauce; the ideal food would be fish, chicken or pork cooked in the simplest way.

Meursault is the next *commune*. Its wine has a lovely green-golden colour, very dry and at the same time soft and mellow, with a delicate and perfumed bouquet. I find it very suitable for most Chinese food.

Another great white burgundy is Corton-Charlemagne, a wine with a firm body but not quite so soft as Meursault. All these wines are made from the Pinot Chardonnay grape (the lesser white burgundies are made from the Aligoté), and they need only two or three years in the bottle before they are ready for drinking. But remember, the greater the wine, the longer its staying power. Also a matured wine becomes softer and more harmonious as it develops what is known as 'bottle age', which shows up as a 'honeyed' quality in most white wines.

Corton-Charlemagne is situated in Aloxe-Corton, a *commune* more noted for its red wines. Le Corton and Clos du Roi are the two best-known vineyards; their wines are firm and mellow, but usually cost less than other well-known burgundies, which makes them better value.

We are now in the heart of burgundy country, with Beaune, Pommard, Volnay and Santenay to the south, and Nuits-St Georges, Vosne-Romanée, Flagey-Échezeaux, Vougeot, Chambolle-Musigny, Gevrey-Chambertin and Morey-St Denis to the north.

All these are *commune* names, some with their best-known vineyard names added on to distinguish themselves. For example, Gevrey is the name of the village, Chambertin is the vineyard. This at first sight rather complicated way of naming wines is well explained in what I regard as the best book on the subject: *Wine* by Hugh Johnson (Mitchell Beazley). Even if you do not intend to take up wine drinking seriously, I still urge you to get a copy of this book. It is sheer joy just to read it through, with or without a glass at hand.

Some experts claim they can distinguish each individual vineyard from each *commune*, all I can say is good luck to them. It seems to be a rather pointless exercise as far as I am concerned. Of course there are differences between each individual wine, but the differences are so subtle and in some cases so varied that it is impossible to generalise. Still less important is to choose a particular wine for a particular dish. I would stick my neck out and declare that *all* red burgundies are excellent accompaniment for *all* Chinese food, seafood included. Having said that, I must qualify my statement somewhat by further declaring that certain dishes (not necessarily seafood) will go particularly well with a white wine.

Take the famous dish, Peking duck, for example. I always used to drink a red wine with it, and thought it was an excellent partnership until the other day, when a friend served a chilled Puligny-Montrachet at his dinner—the effect was sensational! Never before had I experienced such a wonderful flavour, which lingered on in the mouth, with a combination of such richness and subtlety. A true Franco-Chinese entente, you might call it.

I mentioned earlier that in China, it is not the natural taste of the food, but rather the method it is cooked that determines the order of its appearance at the table; therefore you start off with light dishes, then go on to heavier and richer ones. This makes it convenient to serve a lighter wine first, be it white or red, then go on to a more robust and full-bodied wine with a richer flavour. For instance, at a recent dinner, I served a young Pouilly-Vinzelles with cold sliced chicken and deep fried prawn balls; this was followed by a three-year-old Morgon, to go with sesame seed prawn toast, beef in oyster sauce, diced chicken breast and stir-fried kidney flowers. I also opened a 1966 Chambolle-Musigny, which had a great delicacy and finesse with a superb bouquet, whereas the Morgon was lighter with a delightful fruitiness. After the soup came the 'big' dishes: fragrant pork and red-cooked fish. We drank a 1959 Clos de Vougeot, which was soft, supple and elegant, with an aromatic bouquet. Some people may be horrified at the idea of drinking a Clos de Vougeot with fish, but this particular dish had such a rich sauce that no ordinary white wine would have been robust enough to partner it perfectly.

On another occasion, we started with a Riesling from Alsace for the cold *hors d'oeuvres*; then for the next course, which consisted of stir-fried hot dishes (both fish and meat), we had a four-year-old Juliénas, which had a brilliant purple colour, coupled with a very fruity nose, rich in taste and had the quality of 'plumpness' which normally could only be found in a great burgundy. This turned out to be a perfect prelude to our next wine, a 1964 Bonnes Mares; though over ten years old, it had a deep ruby colour, flowery bouquet, with an exceptional finesse, combining body with strength. We all agreed that it was such a lively wine that it still had a long way to go before its peak.

Maurice Healy was once quoted as saying that one will only drink four or five bottles of truly first-class burgundy in one's life— and be lucky at that. In that respect I must count myself being really lucky, for I have already had more than my fair share in my short life so far, and at the risk of being accused of greed, am looking forward to many more great bottles still to come.

The most memorable bottle I ever had was in 1974 at the hospitable table of Mr and Mrs S. K. Ho, two family friends, who opened a 1959 Richebourg, Domaine de la Romanée-Conti, to go with a roast duck with stuffings and several other wonderful dishes. I have no doubt about the excellence and deliciousness of the food, as Mrs Ho is a first-class cook, but to be honest, all I can remember today is the Richebourg. What a velvety softness, combined with a rich fragrance that lingered on long afterwards. Its distinctive flavour was fascinating and impossible to describe. 'Magnificent' was the one word that immediately came to mind.

Bordeaux

With claret, the English word for red Bordeaux, things are much less complicated. To start with more than six times as much wine is produced in the Gironde each year than in the Côte d'Or, also most holdings are large in size, plus the fact that compared with burgundy, the system of *apellation contrôlée* in Bordeaux is simple. Therefore genuine claret of good quality is easily available in abundance, sometimes even at very reasonable prices.

What is the difference in taste between a claret and a burgundy? The answer is very little. They are the two greatest red wines in the world, and the differences are very subtle and therefore difficult to define. Some people will tell you that claret is a light, delicate and dry wine, while burgundy is heavy, rich and sweet. This generalisation makes it sound as though they were two entirely different wines. Far from it—if you compare the two wines of the same quality, you will find there are more similarities between them than, say, between a so-called Spanish 'burgundy' and the genuine thing.

No true wine lover could honestly declare that one is a better wine than the other; it is purely a matter of personal preference. At a blind tasting it is extremely hard even for the experts to distinguish the two wines. Cyril Ray, in his highly entertaining *In a Glass Lightly* (Methuen), unfortunately now out of print, recounted the story about how Harry Waugh, a legendary character in the wine trade for his skill and judgement as a taster, was once asked whether he had ever mistaken a burgundy for a claret, gave the rueful reply: 'Not since luncheon.'

When I mentioned earlier in this book that although I have a personal preference for claret over burgundy, practical experience has taught me that the latter seems to have more affiliation with Chinese food than its cousins from Bordeaux. Perhaps I should have given a reason for my rather bold statement. As you are aware, if you drink a claret with seafood, it leaves a slight metallic taste in your mouth that will spoil both the food and wine for some people; and also most clarets are too elegant and delicate for a richly flavoured dish. But there is still plenty of Chinese food that will partner claret very well, particularly the simply prepared light dishes, not forgetting that wines from St Émilion and Pomerol are much more full-bodied and generous than Médoc—they have been called the burgundies of the Gironde.

One of the commonest mistakes some people make when they complain that claret tastes sour and hard is that they drink the wine long before it is ready. Unlike a burgundy, which takes an average five to six years to mature, and will become drinkable within three or four years of the vintage, a claret will take much longer to reach its peak, and while it is being matured, it is never quite so drinkable as a burgundy of the same age; it will not have much nose nor flavour, it will taste sour and hard because it has no balance of acidity and tannin, which protects the young wine and helps its development to maturity. A high-quality claret of a good vintage will take at least ten years to mature; it will then have a powerful and distinctive bouquet, a fine, fruity flavour with real depth. It will be a *great* wine of overwhelming beauty that tends to linger in your glass even when it has been drained to the last drop.

Not wanting to appear to boast, I have tasted many bottles of great clarets in my time, and they are too numerous to list here. But everyone has his or her favourite *commune* or Château, and if I were asked to state mine, then I must confess that I always have a soft spot for wines from Pomerol, which although bordering on St Émilion, are quite different in that they are more mellow and have a finer bouquet than their neighbours.

Before leaving Bordeaux, a brief mention must be made about its white wines. In Britain, bottles simply labelled 'Bordeaux Blanc' are usually fairly light and medium-dry, those labelled as 'Graves' should be fuller in body, and again tend to be medium-dry or even verging on sweet. But if you drink a four- or five-year-old Château wine, you will find it has a delicious nose, is invariably dry with a big and firm body, and therefore is ideal for a number of Chinese dishes.

As for the sweet wines from Sauternes and Barsac, I do not regard myself as a qualified person to pass any judgement on them. But I do recall drinking the great Château d'Yquem on a number of occasions, and do agree with the connoisseurs that a matured Sauternes has a voluptuous nose, and a full-bodied lusciousness. It is at its best when served with strawberries or peaches, but there are people who would drink it with savoury food throughout a meal. *Chacun a son goût!*

Champagne

Some people regard champagne as the perfect wine to accompany all Chinese food. Much as I like champagne, to serve it throughout a meal is unfair to both the wine and the food. For the past few years, several friends and I have been meeting regularly once a month to taste wines, usually with very simple food. In order to celebrate our first anniversary, we decided to have a 'little feast' with vintage champagne as our theme. There were fourteen of us and we had no less than nine different marques of various vintages. We started off with soya chicken, sesame seed prawn toast, 'smoked' fish, and pork and vegetables—that was fine; next we had Peking duck—I think by then we already would have liked a change of wine; so by the time we came to the last course, fragrant pork and sweet and sour fish, I just had to open a couple of good old (or rather young) Beaujolais, and what a delight it turned out to be!

Good champagne has an incomparably fresh and delicate taste, a beautifully fruity bouquet. Without a doubt, it is the best apéritif in the world. But imitations are quite different. There are a number of good sparkling wines made in other parts of France and indeed throughout the world, but they have nothing like the delicacy nor the firmness of a good champagne. I am not being a wine snob, but if you compare them, side by side, you will immediately tell the difference.

Loire

Perhaps it is not surprising, therefore, that the better sparkling wines are those made by *méthode champenoise*, of which Loire produces the best examples. At a dinner party given by a well-known Chinese gourmet in London, the menu included 'smoked' fish, chicken with mushrooms, roast duck, red-cooked pork and several other dishes, and a sparkling Saumur was followed by a Bourgueil. I must say that neither wine has ever tasted so good to me before. The rather rich food seemed to bring out a pronounced fruity bouquet from the Bourgueil and a fresh acidity from the Saumur, which made the combination into a perfect harmony.

While we are in the Loire Valley, I must mention two of my favourite white wines: Muscadet and Pouilly Fumé. The first is light, fresh and always dry, particularly good with shellfish and sea-food; the second one is more fruity with a distinctive flavour, also dry (not to be confused with Pouilly Fuissé from Mâcon). Both should be drunk young, but I had an eight-year-old Pouilly Fumé once and it was the best one I had ever tasted.

Alsace

Professor Saintsbury found that, despite the wonderful first taste, both hock and Moselle had an 'overpowering and almost barbaric volume of flavour'. Such an accusation cannot be brought against the Alsatian wines, which are dry and firm. I do not wish to dispute with the experts' view that Germany produces the greatest white wines in the world (they certainly are the most expensive), but you must agree that compared with French white wines, most German wines taste rather weak, in spite of their powerful, flowery scent. This delicacy makes them unsuitable for most Chinese food. But the wines of Alsace are spicy and aromatic, at the same time full-bodied with a fruity flavour which is clean-cut. They go particularly well with the rich and strongly flavoured Chinese dishes.

It is very rare to see the name of a vineyard or *commune* on the label of an Alsatian wine. It is usually identified by the grape from which it was made, such as Sylvaner, Riesling, Gewürztraminer and Muscat. The Sylvaner produces a light, fresh and fruity wine, which is excellent as an apéritif; a Riesling is firmer in body and finer in flavour, when well made, it should have a perfect balance of strength and delicacy. I generally find the Gewürztraminer a little overpowering in its spicy scent as well as its strong taste; but the Muscat, though also highly scented, is more crisp and has a clean, dry finish. They all make an ideal introduction to red burgundies at the table, while the white burgundies should precede clarets.

Rhône

Another white wine that is strong, both in alcohol and flavour, and therefore ideal for accompanying most Chinese food, comes from the Rhône Valley. The most famous white Rhône must be Château Grillet, which is extremely expensive, but I only tasted it once and was not impressed. Personally, I would rather pay much less for a white Hermitage or St Joseph, both of which are 'big' wines with plenty of depth—the white Châteauneuf-du-Pape I find less refined, though very strong, like the red.

Red Rhône wines are very popular partly because they represent the best value for money. But you have to choose your plain Côtes du Rhône very carefully as they vary quite a bit. I think that wines that are bottled by the grower himself are usually safest. Otherwise pay a little extra for a *commune* wine such as Hermitage or Côte Rôtie; both are robust and full of character with the latter slightly softer and lighter. These and Châteauneuf-du-Pape, the biggest of them all, should really be left to mature for at least five to eight years in bottle; then they become richer and fuller with a real flavour and scent, like lovely ripe fruit; they will go beautifully with any Chinese food.

I have now practically covered all the major wine areas of France, but they only represent a small proportion of the vast wine industry in France. Do not overlook the *Vins de Pays*, particularly the VDQS (*Vins délimités de qualité supérieure*) such as Costiéres du Gard, Corbiéres, Côtes du Roussillon and Côtes de Provence to name just a few. I notice that Côtes de Ventoux has been upgraded to full *appellation controlée* recently, which is entirely deserved. I should also single out the red wines from Bandol, not far from Marseilles. Each time I go to the Midi, I always make a point of stopping there in order to select a few bottles to bring back to England. I find them excellent with most Chinese dishes.

Readers will have gathered that I am evidently a Francophile as far as taste in wine is concerned. I hasten to add that I do drink and have enjoyed wines from other countries, only I do not feel I know enough about any of them to do justice to them. Perhaps I should just mention that I find some Italian wines wonderful value; besides the famous Chianti Classico, names I remember are Barolo, Bardolino, and Valpolicella for red, Frascati and Soave for white.

I have also enjoyed wines from the Napa Valley in California. Undoubtedly the best one is a white called Pinot Chardonnay, named after the burgundy grape from which it is made. It is crisp and dry, full of scent and fruit, a truly great wine. The best red I have tasted is Cabernet Sauvignon (the principal red grape of Bordeaux); it is not unlike a good claret, with plenty of body and flavour, except, because of the lack of Merlot and other grapes, it is not so mellow. In comparison, the Pinot Noir (the noble red grape of Burgundy) is less successful, though it is still a good wine. Here again, I feel I have not sampled enough varieties to make any fair comment on a great wine district.

If you find that your favourite wine or wines have not even been mentioned by me in this book, do not take my negligence as a sign of disapproval, or lack of appreciation. As I stated earlier, it is not my intention (nor within my capability) to write a comprehensive chapter on all the great wines of the world.

When you drink wine, sheer pleasure should be your prime motivation; the facts that it increases the enjoyment of food, facilitates your digestion and thereby improves your health, and so on, are undoubtedly true, but I rather suspect people who try to justify their reasons for drinking wine—they must secretly have a guilt complex. Like sex, wine is one of the pleasures of life that you do not need to have an excuse for. 'Wine, women and song!' Give me them any day!

But like all good things in life, excessive and indiscriminate application is to be positively avoided. Therefore a few basic points in regard to selecting and serving wine should be observed in order to enhance its enjoyment. One need not be too dogmatic about the 'rules', such as they are, but should use one's own common sense and imagination. Trial and error is a much better way of gaining experience.

Having bought your wine one way or another, be it of high

quality or *vin ordinaire*, treat it with respect. Unless it is to be consumed within a short time, say two or three weeks, the bottle or bottles should be stored in a dark, cool place, horizontally. Avoid any vibration or sudden change of temperature. That is why an underground cellar is an ideal place for storage of wine. But how many of us have cellar space nowadays? Nevertheless, an even temperature is more important than coolness; only bear in mind that wines stored in a warm place will mature more quickly.

All white wine, sherry and champagne included, should be served slightly chilled. If it is served too cold, much of the bouquet and flavour will be lost. Most red wine should be served at room temperature. This is best attained by standing the bottle in the dining-room for twenty-four hours or more, hence the term *chambré*. But under no circumstances should the bottle be immersed in hot water or placed in front of a fire. Such acts are detrimental to any wine.

Always serve your wine in clear glasses: one cannot appreciate the brilliant colour of wine in coloured glasses. Use large glasses, but never fill them to the brim. One cannot appreciate the subtle bouquet if the glass is too full.

Now there only remains the actual drinking of the wine, the joy of which is entirely yours. But I do hope that it will not spoil your enjoyment of it if I leave you with the advice given by an Imperial Physician of the Yuan Dynasty, in the earliest existing Chinese cookery book entitled *Yin Shau Cheng Yao (The Correct Guide to Drinks and Food)*, and first published in 1330. In the chapter on wine, the following points are to be noted:

Do not over-indulge yourself when drinking wine.

If you must get drunk, do not be dead drunk otherwise you will feel ill for the rest of your life.

Do not drink wine continuously: it is bad for your stomach.

When drunk, do not ride a horse or jump about: you may injure yourself.

When drunk, do not have sexual intercourse, it will give you a spotty face in a mild case, or worse still, diarrhoea and piles.

When drunk, do not lose your temper or shout loudly.

When drunk, do not fall asleep in draughts.

Never drink wine without food.

Avoid sweet food with wine.

Do not lift heavy weights if drunk.

Do not take a bath if drunk, it will give you an eye ailment.

If you have an eye infection, avoid getting drunk and eating garlic at the same time. [Well!]

There is certainly quite a lot of sound advice here, but I fail to see any logic in some of them! Anyway, you have now been warned.

APPENDIX I
The Art of Tea Drinking

It is a curious fact that tea and wine drinking do not seem to go together. Yet the enjoyment of both lie in appreciation of the three basic essences: colour, fragrance and flavour. Li Yü, the seventeenth-century Chinese epicure-poet, stated quite categorically in his book on the art of living that great drinkers of tea are not fond of wine, and vice versa. Being a wine lover myself, I feel, therefore, unqualified to talk about the art of tea drinking as we know it in China.

In my family, my grandmother had a great capacity for wine, but treated tea merely as a thirst-quenching beverage; whilst my grandfather, a teetotaller, was a true tea connoisseur. I used to accompany him to the tea shops to select his favourite tea—in China, we have shops that sell nothing but tea, rather like an old-fashioned wine merchant in England, and where a customer is usually treated with respect and courtesy.

A Chinese tea connoisseur attaches great importance to the preparation in tea making, particularly the type of water used. It is generally agreed that mountain spring water is best, river water second, well water third. Water from the tap, being contaminated

with metal, is most unsatisfactory. Similarly never use a brass or any other metal kettle; the ideal one is made of earthenware. Avoid using damp firewood, on account of the smoke, always use freshly boiled water and so on. And of course the most important of all, the tea itself. I think it is true to say that there are almost as many varieties of tea in China as there are wines in France, and there are a great number of books and treatises on tea in China (the earliest in existence being *Ch'a Ching* by Lu Yü, first published in the eighth century).

Some people find tea an ideal substitute for apéritif before a meal —particularly in the middle of the day if you want to cut down your alcoholic intake. It certainly helps to clean your palate; and after a good Chinese meal, nothing is more refreshing than a large pot of hot tea—clear, pale and golden (the kind known as green tea), not the dark red tea which you have to drink with milk and sugar.

APPENDIX II
Chinese Provision Stores

There are a great number of Chinese provision stores (sometimes called Emporiums) in big cities throughout the country, both in England and America. They usually centre around a district known as Chinatown, such as Gerrard Street in London and Nelson Street in Liverpool. If you live too far from a Chinese store, then write to the Mail Order Department of Cheong-Leen Supermarket, 4–10 Tower Street, London, WC2. They do not have a price list, but will give you a quotation for any item you require. There is no point in telephoning them unless you are fluent in Cantonese dialect; otherwise you may cause unnecessary misunderstanding, and thereby harm Anglo-Chinese friendship!

Index

All recipes are shown in italics

Index